A Guidebook to Virginia's African American Historical Markers

A Guidebook to Virginia's African American Historical Markers

Compiled by JENNIFER R. LOUX

MATTHEW S. GOTTLIEB *and*

JAMES K. HARE

with foreword by

COLITA NICHOLS FAIRFAX

Published by the

VIRGINIA DEPARTMENT OF HISTORIC RESOURCES

Distribution by the

UNIVERSITY OF VIRGINIA PRESS

CHARLOTTESVILLE AND LONDON

About this Book

This Guidebook to Virginia's African American Historical Markers *is a publication of the Virginia Department of Historic Resources (DHR), produced in commemoration of the 400th anniversary of the arrival of the first known people from Africa in present-day Virginia—a group of Angolans taken against their will by the Spanish who were subsequently captured from the* San Juan Bautista *by English privateers and landed at Point Comfort in August 1619. It contains the texts of more than 300 markers, relaying information about events, people, and places of statewide or national importance. DHR hopes that the book's reception will warrant later, updated editions as new markers are erected across the state. It is distributed by the University of Virginia Press.*

Frontispiece

An early 1930s photograph of poet Anne Bannister Spencer (1882-1975), who was affiliated with the black literary and cultural movement of the 1920s known as the Harlem Renaissance. She stands before a fountain in her garden with her husband, Edward Spencer, and their two grandchildren. At their feet (center) is a fountain head the Spencers named Prince Ebo, a gift from W. E. B. Dubois during one of his visits. To the right of Prince Ebo is the family's pet crow Joe. The Spencers created at their residence on Pierce Street in Lynchburg a literary and intellectual salon open to many new and old visitors and friends traveling through Lynchburg who could not lodge at the city's "whites only" motels or hotels. (Photo courtesy of Anne Spencer Memorial Foundation)

Contents

Foreword

In late August of 1619, about 20 Africans arrived on the ship *White Lion* at Point Comfort in present-day Hampton. The purpose for those Africans' presence in the Virginia colony was to work and create profits to advance English dominion in the New World. Although a war would be fought in the following century to liberate the colonies from British rule, people of African descent would not be free from home-grown tyranny for many more decades to come. Generations of Americans of African descent have contributed to the physical and philosophical landscape of Virginia and the United States for 400 years, often at great personal peril, loss, and risk. Therefore, the documentation of the events, sacrifices, and personalities that chronicle this quadricentennial trek is an intrinsic task of any society that seeks to recognize both its triumphant and its painful past.

The Historical Highway Marker Program in Virginia is an excellent example of one such effort—in fact the first program of its type to be established in the United States. The Virginia Department of Historic Resources, which administers the program along with the Virginia Department of Transportation, acknowledges that the several hundred markers focused specifically on African Americans that have been erected to date are but a fraction of the inventory of more than 2,600 markers that have been created since 1927. Obviously, Virginia's obligation to a history that owes so much to the contributions made by its African American citizens is far from complete, and in many ways redemptive change has only just begun. Fortunately, the concerted effort to add more African American historical markers remains a high priority of the commonwealth, and the Department of Historic Resources works diligently to ensure that each African American historical marker shares the important mission of all markers in the inventory—that of teaching readers that this particular history is significant and worthy of being remembered.

Today there are several hundred markers that highlight vibrant personalities and illuminate unique aspects of this rich and diverse culture. Examples that come to mind are the birthplace of Carter Godwin Woodson—the Father of Black History; the arduous craft of skilled African American oystermen; the slave revolt in 1831 led by Nat Turner; the founding

Maggie Lena Walker, the first woman to found a bank in the United States. (National Park Service)

of what would become Virginia Union University in 1865; and the Lynchburg medical doctor, Robert Walter Johnson, who trained tennis champions Althea Gibson and Arthur Ashe. There are markers that chronicle beloved communities that birthed strong people who dared to outpace a society that so often rejected them, such as Jackson Ward in Richmond, Israel Hill near Farmville, Josephine City in Berryville, and Free State in Albemarle County. There are also markers that chronicle the achievements of African American women, such as Janie Porter Barrett, Amaza Lee Meredith, Virginia Estelle Randolph, Lucy Diggs Slowe, and Anne Spencer—all notable pioneers in their chosen fields. These are just a few examples of how Virginia's markers showcase the indefatigable spirit of a people who refused to accept societal limitations and tropes, and chose instead to embrace their humanity and direct it to a higher calling.

This year the commonwealth erected the first marker for the victim of a lynching. Mr. Isaac Brandon, of Charles City County, was a married father of eight who was denied the due process of a trial with a competent lawyer before he was murdered. Lynching, a lawless, premeditated and tortuous form of execution, typically consisted of the use of a rope to block the blood flow to the brain by crushing the pharynx and larynx of the victim. This violent act often followed the inhumane beating of the victim by a mob, frequently attracted thousands of people to witness the criminal act of terror, enacted political and economic retaliation toward African American leaders, intimidated families and entire communities from continuing to establish their own self-sufficiency, and denied the civil accommodations afforded to all Americans guaranteed by the Constitution. The families of lynching victims often lost their land, possessions, and other valuables, which were never to be recovered.

The national Equal Justice Initiative has an active program to document and mark the more than 4,000 racial-terror lynchings that occurred in the United States. It is significant, however, and wholly appropriate that Virginia has proceeded on its own to acknowledge its participation in this shameful chapter of American history by documenting the lynching of Isaac Brandon. Sadly, this essential effort will not be complete until each of the 80 or more known locations of racial terror lynchings that occurred in Virginia are acknowledged through the Historical Highway Marker Program.

As a 7th or 8th generation Virginian on my mother's side, I have an intimate relationship with the African American history of the commonwealth. I carry a collective cultural memory of stories that my grandparents and great-grandparents shared about the historic communities of Quioccasin, Ziontown, and Westwood in Henrico County. In my mind, I have met the same people they had the pleasure of meeting, such as Maggie Lena Walker, Rev. John Jasper, and John Mercer Langston. Through my family connections, I have actually met civil rights attorneys Oliver Hill, Sr. and Spottswood William Robinson, III, and civil rights activists and ministers Wyatt Tee Walker and Walter Fauntleroy. Remembering is not only a recollection of dates and facts, it is the ritual of consistently recognizing those whose sacrifices have allowed you to do the work you have intended for your life, so that you, too, can leave your footprint on the earth. Remembering allows you to walk in a blueprint not always made plain on paper. Remembering reminds you of just how powerful people can be when they surpass man-made boundaries and demonstrate the enormous love they have for their communities through their effort to create change. Remembering reminds you that your own life is just a chapter in a greater history of a people and a culture.

The Virginia Department of Historic Resources' capable staff and the Board of Historic Resources, on which I am proud to serve, are unwavering in their efforts to uncover the history of all Virginians and acknowledge that the commonwealth is nothing if not an accumulation of many diverse cultures. Each has an extraordinary story to share. Each cultural group deserves a special place on the boulevards, streets, highways, and rural roads of Virginia where we can remember, and through the noble responsibility of explaining the historical terrain to those who read our markers, we find ourselves again and again in history.

COLITA NICHOLS FAIRFAX, PH.D.
Vice-Chair
Virginia Board of Historic Resources

An unidentified Tuskegee Airman standing on an airfield, looking at planes, Ramitelli, Italy. Photo by Toni Frissell. Virginia's Tuskegee Airmen, including Howard Baugh, Andrew Maples, Jr., Charles B. Smith, and William H. Walker were among the more than 140,000 African Americans who served in the racially segregated U.S. Army Air Forces during World War II. (Library of Congress)

Introduction

VIRGINIA'S HISTORICAL HIGHWAY MARKER PROGRAM
AND AFRICAN AMERICAN HISTORY

As Virginia entered the age of the automobile in the 1920s, the state government looked for ways to channel enthusiasm about the new mode of transportation into widespread economic development. Virginia invested in expanding its highway system and, in 1926, established the Commission of Conservation and Development. The Commission, which sought to fill the roadways with motorists eager to explore Virginia's natural and historic resources, hired historian H. J. Eckenrode to develop a program for marking Virginia's historic sites. By linking important events to the landscape where they had taken place, these markers would turn the commonwealth into an open-air museum, guiding travelers on their journeys. The first markers, most with texts just one or two sentences long, were installed late in 1927 along U.S. Rte. 1 between Richmond and Alexandria. The now-iconic design of Virginia's markers was patented in 1928.

The Conservation Commission no doubt conceived the marker program with a white audience in mind. Eckenrode envisioned carloads of tourists visiting areas both urban and rural, where they would contribute to local economies by stopping for lunch, fueling their automobiles, and perhaps spending the night in a motel or hotel. Participation in this endeavor required not only access to a car, but also confidence that travel in unfamiliar places would be safe and convenient. While the open road promised freedom and adventure to white motorists, African Americans had reason to find automobile tourism much less inviting. Segregation and racial prejudice meant that black travelers were often denied service at roadside businesses or were served on an unequal basis. These conditions, in Virginia and beyond, eventually gave rise to privately published travel guides such as *The Negro Motorist Green Book*, which informed African Americans which public accommodations would admit them.

The white audience, as Eckenrode almost certainly imagined it, also shaped decisions about which subjects would be featured on markers, resulting in a program heavily weighted toward colonial churches and houses, the Revolutionary War, the Civil War, and westward expansion, all with an emphasis on "great men." These were the same topics that academic historians then considered worthy of study. Only three of the 700 markers erected before 1930 dealt explicitly with African American history. One of these highlighted a hospital "for the treatment of mental disease in the negro" (Central State Hospital I-6). Another described Nat Turner's rebellion, which "cost the lives of about sixty whites" (Southampton Insurrection U-122), and the third marker recognized the "faithful slaves" who hid white people during Turner's "servile insurrection" (Buckhorn Quarters U-115). In the same years, only seven markers focused on women of any race (typically wives or relatives of famous men) and, although Virginia Indians appeared frequently in marker texts, they were often described as "heathens" or "savages." Meanwhile, Civil War topics, primarily battles and troop movements, accounted for fully one third of the first 700 markers.

Almost 1,500 markers had been erected by 1941, when the program was suspended during World War II. By then the system of historical signs had won positive attention around the country. Yet in 1948, during a downsizing of state government, Governor William Tuck effectively discontinued the marker program. His staff praised the project for accomplishing its goals and asserted that the addition of new signs could only detract from the "prestige of the significant markers already in the system." In the opinion of a committee of professional historians, "the saturation point in the historical marker system has about been reached." By then, only nine markers mentioned African Americans at all, mostly in brief references, although a marker for Booker T. Washington's birthplace had been erected in Franklin County.

The marker program, in much pared-down form, was folded into the Virginia State Library in 1950. In 1966 the program was transferred to the newly established Virginia Historic Landmarks Commission (forerunner of the present-day Department of Historic Resources, or DHR). Only about 100 new signs were erected between 1950 and 1980, and state funding for new markers was discontinued in 1976.

At that point, the program began accepting applications for highway markers from the public, as it does today. Individuals, historical societies, heritage associations, alumni groups, churches, student organizations, and local governments began applying for markers. To be eligible for a marker, an event, person, or place must be of regional, statewide, or national significance; subjects of strictly local importance do not qualify. The subject must have attained its significance at least fifty years ago, and a marker may not focus on a living person. Modern marker texts are about 100 words long. DHR's purpose in erecting markers is not to honor or memorialize a subject, but rather to educate the public. Successful applicants are required to pay for the manufacture of the signs they have proposed. The Virginia Department of Transportation (VDOT) installs and maintains markers in its right-of-way, while public works departments perform this work in independent localities.

The application system led to the revival of the marker program, and to the inclusion of a much greater variety of topics, beginning early in the 1980s. The definition of what qualified as "historic" expanded during this period, as a new generation of scholars raised awareness of social and cultural history, prominently including the lives of African Americans. Today the marker program is thriving, with 40-50 new texts approved annually. Over the past five years (March 2014– June 2019), 40 percent of all new markers have focused on African American history. Many of these markers pertain to Reconstruction-era churches, Rosenwald Schools, or segregated high schools.

While the application system now sustains the marker program, federal grants received between 1996 and 2009 have also provided crucial support. These funds

The historical marker for African American civil rights leader Dorothy Height was erected in Blackwell, the Richmond neighborhood where she was born, in March 2019. Participants included Governor Ralph S. Northam, First Lady Pamela Northam, Lieutenant Governor Justin E. Fairfax, Board of Historic Resources Vice-Chair Colita N. Fairfax, and a host of dignitaries including the local leadership of Delta Sigma Theta Sorority, Inc., and the National Council of Negro Women — two organizations with which Height is inseparably linked. Marker SA-87. (Marc Wagner, Department of Historic Resources)

enabled DHR to replace some of the oldest markers with updated versions based on modern scholarship, and to create new markers about African Americans, Native Americans, and women. Markers erected under this program include those concerning Anthony Burns, Dorothy Height, Oliver White Hill Sr., the 23rd U.S. Colored Troops, and the Virginia Voters League.

Although the marker program has been moving steadily toward a more accurate and comprehensive treatment of Virginia's history, there is still much work to do. As of 2019, only about 12 percent of the markers in the system were primarily about African Americans. Yet these 300 markers, taken together, finally constitute the critical mass necessary to begin revealing broad patterns about Virginia's past. Anyone who regularly pulls over to look at markers on the roadside will read, again and again, that enslaved people resisted bondage by escaping to the British during the Revolutionary War and the War of 1812, and by fighting for the Union during the Civil War; that African Americans withdrew from biracial churches after 1865 and established their own congregations, with their own leaders; that parents and community members struggled for better schools in the 20th century; that women engaged in community uplift; that entrepreneurs established vibrant businesses; that people of all ages fought for civil rights; and that it took many years after the *Brown v. Board* decision for Virginia to desegregate its public schools.

The modern-day marker program does not avoid difficult subjects. In September 2018, the Board of Historic Resources approved the first marker in Virginia to address a racial lynching, which describes the murder of Isaac Brandon in Charles City County in 1892. In Danville, the marker about Bloody Monday recounts an attack by police on a nonviolent civil rights demonstration in 1963. In Lynchburg, the marker about Ota Benga (ca. 1885–1916) tells the story of an African man who was brought to the United States and exhibited in a New York zoo alongside an orangutan before dying by suicide in Virginia. While these are painful subjects to confront, ignoring them would perpetuate a dangerously distorted impression of Virginia's and America's past. Virginians of all backgrounds must know the full scope of the state's history if we are to comprehend and address the complex issues that confront us today.

Highway markers are visible to a very large audience, including many people who might have no other occasion to read about Virginia history. The markers bear the state seal, convey a sense of authority, and indicate what Virginians think is important about their history. It is therefore imperative that the marker program continue to correct the willful omissions of its earlier decades and work to inscribe on the landscape a true accounting of Virginia's past—one that recognizes the central role of African Americans in the development of the commonwealth over the last 400 years.

The Virginia Department of Historic Resources: An Overview

The Department of Historic Resources (DHR) traces its origins to 1966, when the General Assembly created its predecessor, the Virginia Historic Landmarks Commission. The agency's mission is to foster, encourage, and support the stewardship of Virginia's significant historic architectural, archaeological, and cultural resources. In addition to managing the historical highway marker program, DHR and its seven-member, governor-appointed Board of Historic Resources oversee Virginia's historic preservation initiatives. DHR formally recognizes significant properties by listing them in the Virginia Landmarks Register, administers a rehabilitation tax credit program, offers an easement process for historic properties, and reviews federal projects for their impact on historic resources. Serving also as Virginia's State Historic Preservation Office in the federal preservation system, DHR nominates properties to the National Register of Historic Places. The agency's archaeologists, architects, architectural historians, archivists, conservators, and historians provide technical assistance to local governments, preservation groups, and owners of historic properties in the interest of preserving Virginia's irreplaceable cultural resources.

Jennifer R. Loux, Ph.D.
Highway Marker Program Manager
June 2019

How to Use the Guidebook

This is the inaugural edition of *A Guidebook to Virginia's African American Historical Markers* and includes more than three hundred markers that have been installed along the roadways of the commonwealth since the program began. The state has been divided into five geographic-cultural regions: Northern Virginia and the Northern Neck (Region 1); Northern Piedmont, Valley, and Western Mountains (Region 2); Central Virginia and Central Piedmont (Region 3); Eastern Virginia (Region 4); and Southern Piedmont, Blue Ridge, and Southwest (Region 5).

Within each of the five sections, the marker text entries are divided according to their locations by county or city and arranged alphabetically by the full name of the marker (Aberdeen Gardens; Booker T. Washington Birthplace; The Anne Spencer House–1313 Pierce Street; United Negro College Fund; West End High School; etc.). In addition to the title of the marker, the location of the sign is provided based on records at the Virginia Department of Transportation and the Department of Historic Resources. The regional format is intended to present an easy approach for visiting a series of markers in an area. An index for properties featured on a marker or mentioned within its text has been provided. A great deal of additional information about the historic properties can be accessed online via the DHR website, www. dhr.virginia.gov. Our website also provides direct access to the available National Register of Historic Places documentation.

The traveler should be aware that there are other historical markers that resemble the state's in shape and design. This book includes only official state historical markers that discuss subjects of particular significance in African American history. Markers about the Civil War—unquestionably a subject of importance to African Americans—are not included here unless they pertain to specific actions by blacks. For example, the reader will find several markers pertinent to the activities of U.S. Colored Troops during the conflict. Markers for the many townships, farms, and historic plantations that exist due to the labor of enslaved African Americans have also been excluded from the *Guidebook* despite the fact that a conscious effort has been made to acknowledge the sacrifice of the enslaved within the texts of respective markers for the past thirty years. For the most part, inclusion in the *Guidebook* has been based on criteria that include individual and collective achievement by Virginians since 1619 to establish independence, secure civil rights, combat injustice, acquire positions of leadership, rise to the highest ranks of professional regard, and in general, to surmount the many barriers that have denied life, liberty, and the pursuit of happiness to so many Americans. The program, however, does not shy from documenting the negative aspects of Virginia's history, and as noted in the foreword, the first marker to recognize an incident of racial terror was erected in Charles City County in 2019.

In most cases, official Virginia historical highway markers measure forty-two by forty inches, although the early signs vary in size. The markers are painted silver and are currently cast in aluminum with black letters. Text usually appears on both sides and ranges from a sentence or two (on the earliest markers erected) to a little over a hundred words today. Each sign also includes the marker's title and the letter-number code identifying it; the Seal of the Commonwealth within a triangle at the top; and, along the bottom, an attribution indicating what state agency approved the sign and when. While the attributions on recent signs read "Department of Historic Resources," earlier markers name predecessor agencies that have managed the program, such as the Department of Conservation and Historic Resources, the Virginia Historic Landmarks Commission, the Virginia State Library, and the Conservation and Development Commission.

When the program was created in the late 1920s, the identification code consisted of a letter that usually referenced a specific road (for example, "E" was given to U. S Rte. 1 markers north of Richmond) and a number, usually in sequential order, that related the signs as part of a specific letter series. Markers are now assigned a letter code that matches the primary code used in the jurisdiction where a sign is erected. Each new marker is given the next number in the series. In a few cases during the early years of the program, the same letter-number code was accidentally assigned to multiple signs.

The signs reveal different styles of writing and punctuation, depending on when they were created. For instance, older signs in Clarke County dropped the "e" at the end of the county's name. The marker texts reveal something of our history, because they reflect the scholarly and social conventions, available documentation, and marker procedures and criteria of the eras in which they were produced.

A few missing or recently damaged signs that have been taken down are listed in the *Guidebook*, as are several that are scheduled to be erected after its publication. For missing or damaged markers, funding is pending to replace them. When markers are replaced, the topics of the texts are thoroughly researched again by historians at DHR

COMMONWEALTH OF VIRGINIA
This state map identifies the guidebook's five
geographic regions; marker texts appear
accordingly in the pages that follow.

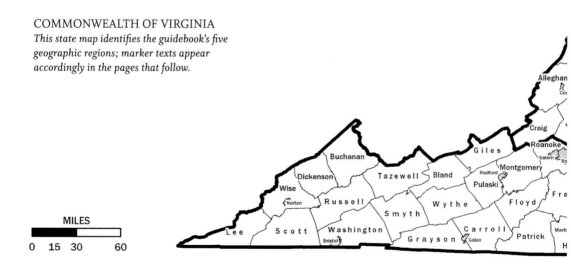

MILES

0   15   30   60

in order to keep them accurate and current. Original and earlier versions of texts are archived and are always available for review upon request. Unfortunately, some markers listed here may disappear over time for various reasons (theft, repairs, destruction, or relocation due to construction). If you fail to locate a marker, if you discover a damaged sign, or if you have questions about a specific marker text, please contact the manager of the Virginia Historical Highway Marker Program at DHR.

The index that appears in this edition is alphabetical, and last names are used when the marker title refers to an individual; e.g. The Anne Spencer House–1313 Pierce Street appears as Spencer House, Anne, The, –1313 Pierce Street. A number of subjects have entries in the index to facilitate a review of particular areas of interest such as abolition, architects, musicians, teachers, sports, etc. DHR's comprehensive online marker database can be accessed at www.dhr.virginia.gov/highway-markers/.

For Information

Virginia Department of Historic Resources
Historical Highway Marker Program
2801 Kensington Avenue
Richmond, VA 23221

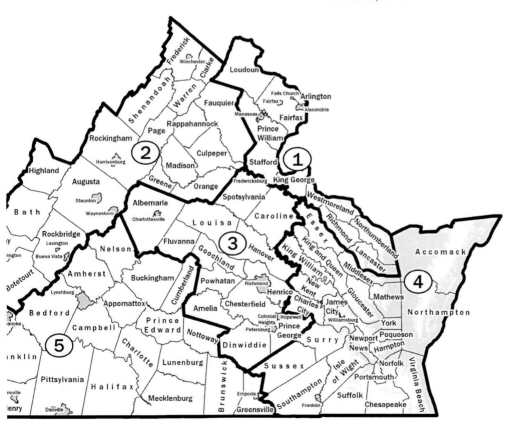

The press room of the Richmond Planet. *Editor-in-chief John Mitchell, Jr., was the forceful voice of the* Richmond Planet *from 1884 until his death in 1929. (Library of Congress)*

A Guidebook to Virginia's African American Historical Markers

Inaugural Edition

Five African American Virginians leave the new Alexandria Library in
1939 after being arrested for attempting to use the segregated facility.
In 1940, Alexandria opened the Robert Robinson Library for African
Americans. Nineteen years later, desegregation of the city's library system
finally began. (Alexandria Black History Museum)

Northern Virginia and the Northern Neck

CITY OF ALEXANDRIA

FAIRFAX COUNTY

CITY OF FALLS CHURCH

KING GEORGE COUNTY

LANCASTER COUNTY

LOUDOUN COUNTY

NORTHUMBERLAND COUNTY

PRINCE WILLIAM COUNTY

RICHMOND COUNTY

STAFFORD COUNTY

WESTMORELAND COUNTY

CITY OF ALEXANDRIA

E-89   ALEXANDRIA ACADEMY

On S. Washington Street between Wilkes and Wolfe Streets.   On 17 Dec. 1785, George Washington endowed a school here in the recently established Alexandria Academy "for the purpose of educating orphan children." In 1812, an association of free African Americans founded its own school here in space vacated by white students. Young Robert E. Lee attended another school in the Academy from 1818 to 1823, when it closed and the building was sold. During the Civil War the Academy served as a freedman's hospital. Returned to the Alexandria School Board in 1884, the Alexandria Academy was used as a school and administrative facility until 1982. The Historic Alexandria Foundation restored it in 1999.

E-88   ALEXANDRIA LIBRARY SIT-IN

On N. Washington Street between Queen and Princess Streets.   On 21 Aug. 1939, five young African American men applied for library cards at the new Alexandria Library to protest its whites-only policy. After being denied, William Evans, Edward Gaddis, Morris Murray, Clarence Strange, and Otto L. Tucker each selected a book from the shelves, sat down, and read quietly. The men were arrested and charged with disorderly conduct despite their polite demeanor. Local attorney Samuel W. Tucker, who helped plan the protest, represented them in court. The judge never issued a ruling. In 1940, Alexandria opened the Robert Robinson Library for African Americans. Desegregation of the library system began by 1959.

E-124   ALFRED STREET BAPTIST CHURCH

At corner of S. Alfred Street at Duke Street. Alfred Street Baptist Church is home to the oldest African American congregation in Alexandria, dating to the early 19th century. It has served as a prominent religious, educational, and cultural institution. In 1818, the congregation, then known as the Colored Baptist Society, began worship services here in the midst of the Bottoms, a free black neighborhood. By 1820 the church created its educational branch, providing religious and secular opportunities for both black children and adults. In 1855, free black craftsmen probably designed and built the brick church. Alterations to the building occurred in the 1880s and in 1994 the church constructed a new sanctuary.

E-139   BEULAH BAPTIST CHURCH

At 320 S. Washington Street.   African Americans escaping slavery found refuge in Alexandria after Union troops occupied the city in 1861. The Rev. Clement "Clem" Robinson established the First Select Colored School in 1862. Hundreds of students registered for day and evening classes and for courses at the associated Beulah Normal and Theological Institute. In Oct. 1863, Robinson organized Beulah Baptist Church, the first African American church founded in Alexandria after Union occupation. The congregation constructed its brick sanctuary here on the edge of the African American neighborhood known as The Bottoms. The school then moved to this site, and education remained central to Beulah's mission.

E-131   FRANKLIN AND ARMFIELD SLAVE OFFICE (1315 DUKE STREET)

On Duke Street between S. West and S. Payne Streets.   Isaac Franklin and John Armfield leased this brick building with access to the wharves and docks in 1828 as a holding pen for enslaved people being shipped from Northern Virginia to Louisiana. They purchased the building

Rep. John Mercer Langston. Markers E-136 and W-222. (New York Public Library Digital Collections)

and three lots in 1832. From this location Armfield bought bondspeople at low prices and shipped them south to his partner Franklin, in Natchez, Mississippi, and New Orleans, Louisiana, to be sold at higher prices. By the 1830s they often sold 1,000 people annually, operating as one of the largest slave-trading companies in the United States until 1836. Slave traders continuously owned the property until 1861.

E-109 FREEDMEN'S CEMETERY

Intersection of S. Washington Street at Church Street. Federal authorities established a cemetery here for newly freed African Americans during the Civil War. In January 1864, the military governor of Alexandria confiscated for use as a burying ground an abandoned pasture from a family with Confederate sympathies. About 1,700 freed people, including infants and black Union soldiers, were interred here before the last recorded burial in January 1869. Most of the deceased had resided in what is known as Old Town and in nearby rural settlements. Despite mid-twentieth-century construction projects, many burials remain undisturbed. A list of those interred here has also survived.

E-134 L'OUVERTURE HOSPITAL AND BARRACKS

On Prince Street between S. West and S. Payne Streets. Named for Toussaint L'Ouverture, the Haitian revolutionary, L'Ouverture Hospital opened early in 1864 near the Freedmen's barracks in Alexandria to serve sick and injured United States Colored Troops (USCT). Designed by the U.S. Army, the hospital complex could accommodate about 700 patients and occupied the city block just south of here. The hospital also served African American civilians, many of whom had escaped from slavery and sought refuge in Alexandria. In Dec. 1864, more than 400 patients led a successful protest demanding that USCTs be buried in Alexandria National Cemetery, with full honors, rather than at the Contrabands and Freedmen Cemetery.

E-137 PARKER-GRAY HIGH SCHOOL

On Madison Street between N. West and N. Fayette Streets. On this site stood Parker-Gray High School, the first high school for African American students in Alexandria. Before the school was built, African American students had to attend school in the District of Columbia. The noted civil rights attorney Charles Houston and other local activists persuaded the city of Alexandria to appropriate funds to build the school, and it opened in 1950. Because of the 1954 U.S. Supreme Court's *Brown v. the Board of Education* decision, court-ordered desegregation began in 1959. The last class graduated from the high school in 1965. Parker-Gray closed in 1979 as a middle school. The Parker-Gray Historic District bears the school's name.

E-140   ROBERTS MEMORIAL UNITED METHODIST CHURCH

At 606A S. Washington Street.   At the end of the 18th century, African Americans constituted almost half the congregation at Alexandria's Trinity Methodist Episcopal Church. With support from Trinity, black members founded a separate congregation early in the 1830s, and their sanctuary was completed here in 1834. The church, initially known as Davis Chapel, was renamed in 1845 for Bishop Robert Richford Roberts, a former pastor of Trinity. Members quickly established a Sunday school that offered general education and religious training. Frederick Douglass and Booker T. Washington lectured here late in the 19th century. The sanctuary was remodeled in the Gothic Revival style in 1894.

E-136   SHILOH BAPTIST CHURCH

At 1401 Duke Street.   Alexandria, occupied by Union troops during the Civil War, became a refuge for African Americans escaping slavery. Before the war ended, about 50 former slaves founded the Shiloh Society, later known as Shiloh Baptist Church. Members held services in U.S. government buildings until Sept. 1865, when their new frame church on West Street was dedicated. The congregation flourished under the leadership of the Rev. Leland Warring, pastor for more than 20 years. The brick Gothic Revival sanctuary here was completed in 1893. Prominent visitors have included Rep. John Mercer Langston, Dr. Dorothy Height, and Pres. George W. Bush.

E-147   THIRD BAPTIST CHURCH

At 917 Princess Street.   Alexandria, occupied by Union troops in 1861, attracted many African Americans escaping slavery. In Jan. 1864, a group of formerly enslaved people organized Third Freedmen's Baptist Church (later Third Baptist Church).

The congregation moved to this site in 1865 and built its Romanesque Revival sanctuary in the 1890s. The church's first minister was the Rev. George Washington Parker (ca. 1832-1873), who had been free before the Civil War. He worked with the Rev. Clement Robinson to start the First Select Colored School in 1862, was a local Republican Party leader during Reconstruction, and was the first African American member of the Alexandria Common Council.

E-151   UNIVERSAL LODGE NO. 1

At intersection of S. Mt. Vernon and E. Oxford Avenues.   Prince Hall Masonry originated in Massachusetts in 1775 when a lodge attached to the British army initiated Prince Hall and 14 other free black men as Freemasons. Universal Lodge No. 1, the first Prince Hall lodge in Virginia, was established in Alexandria on 5 Feb. 1845. According to tradition, founders William Dudley, Benjamin Crier, and Sandy Bryant were seamen who had become masons in Liverpool, England, in the 1830s. They later joined Social Lodge No. 1 in Washington, DC, and worked to charter a new lodge across the Potomac River. Before the Civil War, Universal Lodge No. 1 met secretly in a house on South Royal Street in Hayti, a black enclave.

FAIRFAX COUNTY

E-94   GUM SPRINGS

On Richmond Highway at Fordson Road. Gum Springs, an African-American community, originated here on a 214-acre farm bought in 1833 by West Ford (ca. 1785-1863), a freed man, skilled carpenter, and manager of the Mount Vernon estate. The freedman's school begun here in 1867 at Bethlehem Baptist Church encouraged black settlement. In 1890 the Rev. Samuel K. Taylor, William

Dorothy Height presenting the Mary McLeod Bethune Human Rights Award to Eleanor Roosevelt, 1960. Markers E-136 and SA-87. (National Archives)

Belfield, Lovelace Brown, Hamilton Gray, Robert D. King, Henry Randall, and Nathan Webb formed the Joint Stock Company of Gum Springs and sold lots. Gum Springs has remained a vigorous black community.

E-146 WOODLAWN METHODIST CHURCH

At 7730 Fordson Road. African Americans in Woodlawn, four miles southwest of here, established Woodlawn Methodist Episcopal Church ca. 1866. The Woodlawn area, formerly part of George Washington's Mount Vernon estate, was home to African Americans who had been free landowners before the Civil War, people recently emancipated from slavery, and northern Quakers who had arrived in the 1840s. The Methodist church, built on land purchased from Quakers, housed a Freedmen's Bureau school that became a public school by 1871. The congregation established a cemetery and in 1888 built a new sanctuary. When Fort Belvoir expanded during World War II, the church moved near here to the historically black community of Gum Springs.

CITY OF FALLS CHURCH

C-91 TINNER HILL

At 106 Tinner Hill Road. An early rural branch of the National Association for the Advancement of Colored People (NAACP) was founded here on Tinner Hill. In 1915, the Town of Falls Church proposed an ordinance to segregate black and white residential sections. Local African Americans formed the Colored Citizens Protective League and fought this ordinance. In 1918, the league became the Falls Church and Vicinity Branch of the NAACP. Meeting in members' homes around Tinner Hill, the branch focused on public education, voter registration, travel regulations, and equal access to public services. Strategies developed by the branch were effectively used in other localities throughout the Civil Rights era.

KING GEORGE COUNTY

EP-10 RALPH BUNCHE HIGH SCHOOL

At 10139 James Madison Parkway (Rte. 301). Ralph Bunche High School was built as a direct result of the Federal District Court case *Margaret Smith et al.*

v. School Board of King George County, Virginia, which was filed in 1947. The judge ruled that jurisdictions should ensure the "equalization" of segregated school facilities for whites and African Americans. White segregationists hoped to avoid integration by constructing "separate but equal" facilities, but the NAACP quickly moved on to demanding the end of segregation altogether. Named after the noted political scientist and diplomat, Ralph Bunche High School opened in 1949 and closed in 1968 after the county desegregated its schools.

LANCASTER COUNTY

J-91   A. T. WRIGHT HIGH SCHOOL

At James Wharf Road (Rte. 637) near intersection with Newtown Road (Rte. 654). Albert Terry Wright (1871-1944) was born in Hanover County, Virginia. He taught in the black schools of Richmond and, by 1908, at White Stone in Lancaster County. By 1921 Wright was principal of the county's first high school for blacks, which was constructed largely with funds raised by black residents. Named in his honor, A. T. Wright High School served black students until 1959, when the county opened Brookvale High School. The history of the man and his school exemplified the struggle for education by Virginia's rural blacks.

J-108   DR. MORGAN E. NORRIS (c. 1883–1966)

At intersection of Mary Ball Road (Rte. 3) and Boys Camp Road.   Dr. Morgan E. Norris, a Lancaster native and the Northern Neck's first black physician, practiced medicine at this site 1917-1964. He opened to all races specialty surgical clinics, bringing enhanced medical care to the lower Northern Neck. In 1928 Dr. Norris led a campaign to build the first brick elementary school for black children in the Northern Neck. In 1939 he spearheaded a boycott to secure free bus transportation for black schoolchildren and led the Northern Neck Progressive Association's annual fair from 1927 until 1957. He was the second black trustee of Hampton University, and the first black coroner in the state.

J-109   69 SLAVES ESCAPE TO FREEDOM

On Mary Ball Road (Rte. 3) approximately 1500 feet north of Robert O. Norris Jr. Bridge.   About 2,400 enslaved African Americans in Virginia escaped to the British during the War of 1812, encouraged in part by a proclamation issued on 2 Apr. 1814 offering them freedom and resettlement in "His Majesty's Colonies." Three enslaved men from Corotoman, a plantation two miles west of here, fled on 18 Apr. 1814. Several days later, they guided British barges back to carry off friends and relatives, including 46 children, the largest group of slaves to leave a Chesapeake Bay plantation during the war. Some settled in Nova Scotia or Trinidad. British reparations later compensated some owners for departed slaves, including, in 1828, those from Corotoman.

LOUDOUN COUNTY

T-28   ASHBURN SCHOOL

On Ashburn Road (Rte. 641) between Stubble Road and Gloucester Parkway.   On this site stands Ashburn Colored School, a one-room public schoolhouse built ca. 1892 for African American students. Virginia's public school system, established in 1870, was racially segregated from its inception. Schools for black children received less funding and offered fewer educational opportunities than those for whites. The U.S. Supreme Court ruled in

Brown v. Board of Education (1954) that segregated schools were unconstitutional, but Virginia's government resisted integration. This school closed in 1958, when its students were transferred to a new segregated school in Leesburg. Loudoun County schools were fully desegregated in the 1968-1969 school year.

F-35   DOUGLASS COMMUNITY SCHOOL

In Leesburg at 407 E. Market Street. Before the construction of this high school, there were no schools beyond 7th grade for black students in Loudoun County. Late in the 1930s, the parent-teacher associations of various black schools formed the County-Wide League to raise money to build a high school. The league hired well-known civil rights attorney Charles H. Houston to help persuade county officials to allocate funds for the new school. In 1941 the league succeeded in obtaining a loan of $30,000 from the State Literary Fund. Named for Frederick Douglass, the noted black abolitionist and orator, the school still serves the county today.

T-47   LOUDOUN COUNTY EMANCIPATION ASSOCIATION GROUNDS

In Purcellville on S. 20th Street (Rte. 611) south of Willie Palmer Way.   The association was organized by African Americans in nearby Hamilton in 1890 to commemorate the preliminary Emancipation Proclamation issued by President Abraham Lincoln on 22 Sept. 1862 and "to cultivate good fellowship, to work for the betterment of the race, educationally, morally and materially." Emancipation Day, or the "Day of Freedom," was celebrated throughout the nation on different days. In 1910, the association incorporated and purchased ten acres of land in Purcellville. More than 1,000 people attended the

annual Emancipation Day activities held here until 1967. The site served as a black religious, social, civic, and recreational center. The property was sold in 1971.

F-103   MT. ZION UNITED METHODIST CHURCH

In Leesburg at 12 North Street NE. Mt. Zion, recognized as the oldest continuing African American Methodist congregation in Virginia, traces its origins to the Old Stone Church, established in Leesburg in 1766. Black members of Old Stone Church, desiring their own church after the Civil War, purchased land here for $250 in 1867 and built Mt. Zion. The Rev. William O. Robey, who taught in schools for emancipated African Americans, led the congregation. From 1939 to 1968, Mt. Zion was part of the segregated Central Jurisdiction of the Methodist Church. Mt. Olive Church, established by African Americans in nearby Gleedsville in 1889, merged with Mt. Zion in 1984-1985.

NORTHUMBERLAND COUNTY

O-69   AFRICAN AMERICANS IN THE WAR OF 1812

At 468 Buzzards Point Road (Rte. 656). During the War of 1812, thousands of enslaved African Americans gained freedom by fighting for the British or serving as guides during British raids on coastal communities. Many were given the choice of enlisting in the armed services or settling in various locations throughout the British Empire. East of here on Tangier Island, at the British base of Fort Albion, the British trained African Americans to serve in the Colonial Marines. From Fort Albion, the Colonial Marines, along with British troops, engaged the Virginia militia in numerous landings along the Northern Neck and the Eastern Shore throughout the summer of 1814. (*Reverse*) Impressment of

Americans into British service and the violation of American ships were among the causes of America's War of 1812 with the British, which lasted until 1815. Beginning in 1813, Virginians suffered from a British naval blockade of the Chesapeake Bay and from British troops' plundering the countryside by the Bay and along the James, Rappahannock, and Potomac rivers. The Virginia militia deflected a British attempt to take Norfolk in 1813, and engaged British forces throughout the war. By the end of the war, more than 2000 enslaved African Americans in Virginia had gained their freedom aboard British ships.

O-70 BRITISH ATTACKS AT KINSALE AND MUNDY POINT

On Hampton Highway (Rte. 202) approximately 100 feet south of intersection with Locust Lane (Rte. 675). Two miles east on 3 Aug. 1814, 500 British marines and seamen under Adm. Sir George Cockburn landed at Mundy's Point and Kinsale. Opposing the enemy at the Point were Capt. William Henderson and thirty Northumberland county militiamen. Henderson's company was forced to retreat to the county courthouse. Later that day, British forces took Kinsale, burned the town, and seized tobacco. Three days later, they began raids along the Coan River. Among the British troops were about fifty formerly enslaved African Americans, who were among the thousands who gained freedom by fighting or working for the British. (Reverse, see O-69).

O-74 FIRST BAPTIST CHURCH

At 3585 Courthouse Road at First Baptist Church. First Baptist Church, the earliest African American Baptist congregation in Northumberland County, originated in 1866 when black members of Coan Baptist Church began holding worship services at the home of Alexander Day. They later worshiped at Howland Chapel School, built just northeast of here in 1867 with funding from New York-born educator, reformer, and philanthropist Emily Howland. Revivals were held under a nearby brush arbor. Led by the Rev. Daniel Payne, pastor for more than 30 years, the congregation erected its first sanctuary here in 1892. The present Gothic Revival-style sanctuary was completed in 1941 under the guidance of longtime pastor Rev. Henry C. Roane.

Holley Graded School. Marker O-48. (DHR 066-0112)

O-73 FREEDOM FOR SLAVES OF ROBERT CARTER III

Near 7013 Northumberland Highway (Rte. 360). On 5 Sept. 1791, Robert Carter III (1728-1804), one of the wealthiest men in the United States, filed a deed of manumission at the Northumberland County Courthouse. This document eventually freed more than 500 enslaved African Americans owned by Carter in several Virginia counties. "To retain them in Slavery," Carter wrote, "is contrary to the true principles of Religion & Justice." The deed, structured to withstand resistance by Carter's heirs and neighbors, liberated slaves gradually in small groups. Because children were freed when they reached adulthood, the manumission took decades to complete. Many of the freed people became tenants on Carter's land.

O-48 HOLLEY GRADED SCHOOL

On Northumberland Highway (Rte. 360) about 1/3 mile east of Glebe Road (Rte. 626). In 1868, Caroline Putnam (1826-1917) established a school for the children of former slaves here. In 1869, her lifelong friend, Sallie Holley (1818-1893) of N.Y., abolitionist and suffragette, purchased this two-acre site. Holley was an agent of the American Anti-Slavery Society from 1851 to 1870. In 1917 this site was deeded to a board of eleven local black trustees. The third school built here was begun in 1914 and completed in 1933 with funds raised solely within the black community. The four-room structure was the largest black elementary school in Northumberland County. Since 1917 Holley Graded School has remained under the trustees' control.

O-61 JULIUS ROSENWALD HIGH SCHOOL

On Northumberland Highway (Rte. 360) just west of Liberty Road (Rte. 726). Originally known as Northumberland County Training School, this institution opened in 1917, under principal John M. Ellison. Local African Americans raised more than $7,000 to build the school and received additional funding from the Rosenwald Fund. Julius Rosenwald, chairman of the board of directors of Sears Roebuck and Co., created this fund in 1917 to finance the building of rural southern schools for blacks. Some 5,000 Rosenwald schools were built in 15 states, including 308 in Virginia. On 12 Nov. 1932, under its principal the Reverend Dr. Henry M. Ruffin, the school was renamed the Julius Rosenwald High School. It closed in 1958.

O-72 THE REV. PAYMUS NUTT (CA. 1817–CA. 1899)

On Richmond Road (Rte. 360) at intersection with Owl Town Road (Rte. 711). The Rev. Paymus (Pyramus) Nutt, born into slavery, helped organize four African American churches in Northumberland County after the Civil War. In 1866 he co-founded First Baptist. Shiloh Baptist, established in 1867, called him to be its first (interim) pastor. He was ordained there and served about 10 years. In 1867 Nutt also became the first pastor of Zion Baptist, Lottsburg, where he served for 25 years. He helped establish Lively Hope Baptist Church in 1880 and was the Northern Neck Baptist Association's first moderator. The Freedmen's Bureau identified Nutt as one of seven local African Americans qualified for office holding under military Reconstruction.

PRINCE WILLIAM COUNTY

G-16 JAMES ROBINSON HOUSE

On Lee Highway (Rte. 29) approximately 1400 feet east of Sudley Road (Rte. 234). To the south stood the farmhouse of James Robinson, a former slave freed by Landon Carter. There, during the First Battle of

James Robinson's house, Manassas National Battlefield Park. Photographed by George Barnard in 1862. Badly damaged by arsonists in 1993 and then destroyed. Marker G-16. (Library of Congress)

Manassas on 21 July 1861, Col. Wade Hampton's Legion covered the Confederates falling back to Henry Hill, where Jackson stood "like a stone wall." The house survived that battle, and during the Second Battle of Manassas in August 1862 served the Union troops as a field hospital. Congress later authorized compensation to Robinson for property damages. The present house stands partially on the foundation of the original.

RICHMOND COUNTY

J-99   NORTHERN NECK INDUSTRIAL ACADEMY

On Rte. 3 at the intersection with Farnham Creek Road.   The Northern Neck Baptist Association established the Northern Neck Industrial Academy in 1898 through financial contributions from local black Baptist churches. The academy opened approximately three miles to the west on Route 608 at Oak Hill Farm in Oct. 1901 as the first high school for blacks in Richmond County. Students from Lancaster, Northumberland,

Westmoreland, King George, and Essex Counties also attended the academy, often living in on-site dormitories. Sunday school and church services took place here as well. The establishment of public county high schools in the early 20th century resulted in its closure by 1938. The property was eventually sold and the main buildings are no longer standing.

STAFFORD COUNTY

E-133   ANTHONY BURNS   (1834-1862)

In Falmouth at 401 River Road.   Anthony Burns was born into slavery near here. In 1854 Burns escaped from Richmond to Boston. His owner demanded his rendition under the Fugitive Slave Act of 1850. Burns's arrest on 24 May 1854 inspired abolitionists to attempt his rescue, but 1,500 troops escorted Burns aboard a revenue cutter to return him to Virginia. The episode increased abolitionist sentiment across the North, with an abolitionist dubbing the affair "the New Crime Against Humanity." Antislavery activists, including African American Bostonians, freed Burns through purchase in 1855, after which he attended Oberlin College. He became a minister and died in Canada West (later Ontario) in 1862.

J-44　BETHLEHEM PRIMITIVE BAPTIST CHURCH AND CEMETERY

At 135 Chapel Green Road (Rte. 602). This church originated in 1868 when 27 African Americans withdrew from nearby White Oak Church and selected the Rev. York Johnson, a former slave, as their pastor. Johnson founded the Union Branch of the True Vine, a mutual aid society, reportedly with the assistance of the Freedmen's Bureau. The church established a cemetery, enabling African Americans to exercise newfound autonomy over burial practices and funerals. Buried here are veterans of World Wars I and II and Korea. The church's sanctuary, built in 1870, was replaced in 1951. Here the Stafford County branch of the NAACP was founded, and community members met to plan strategies for the desegregation of local public schools.

E-231　STAFFORD TRAINING SCHOOL

At 1739 Jefferson Davis Highway (Rte. 1). Stafford Training School, later known as H. H. Poole School, was constructed in 1939 by the Public Works Administration after African American parents raised money to buy the land. During the segregation era, this was the only school in Stafford County offering black students an education beyond seventh grade. After an earlier attempt failed, two young students from this school, Doretha and Cynthia Montague, successfully entered the all-white Stafford Elementary School on 5 Sept. 1961, seven years after the Supreme Court's *Brown v. Board of Education* decision ruled school segregation unconstitutional. Thereafter school systems in the Fredericksburg region desegregated.

WESTMORELAND COUNTY

JT-19　ARMSTEAD TASKER JOHNSON SCHOOL

At the A. T. Johnson Human Services Building on Kings Highway (Rte. 3). The A. T. Johnson High School was built in 1937 in the Colonial Revival style as the first public high school constructed for

Miss Giles's class at H. H. Poole Jr. High School, former Stafford Training School, 1954-55. Marker E-231. (DHR 089-0247)

Bennett McCoy served during the American Revolution with the 15th Virginia Regiment in Virginia and the Carolinas. He was taken prisoner by the British during the Siege of Charleston, depicted here by Alonzo Chappel, until he was exchanged at the end of the war. Marker JT-20. (Brown University)

African Americans in Westmoreland County. The new school was named for Armstead Tasker Johnson (1857-1944), a black educator and community leader of the grassroots effort for its construction. Local African Americans raised money to build the school. Additional financing came from the federal Works Progress Administration, the Jeanes and Slater black education funds, and the Westmoreland County School Board. The school was converted to a junior high school in Sept. 1970 and served as a middle school from Sept. 1990 to June 1998. It was listed on the Virginia Landmarks Register and the National Register of Historic Places in 1998.

JT-21 CHARLES B. SMITH—99TH FIGHTER SQUADRON (TUSKEGEE AIRMEN)

Approximately 1000 feet south of Ferry Landing (Rte. 638) on James Monroe

Highway (Rte. 205). Born in Westmoreland County, Charles Bernard Smith (1917–1991) is one of more than 140,000 African Americans who served in the racially segregated U.S. Army Air Forces during World War II. Trained at Chanute Field, Illinois, in aircraft ground support with the 99th Fighter Squadron, the famed "Tuskegee Airmen," he served in North Africa and Europe as technical sergeant and crew chief. In more than 200 missions as bomber escorts, the Tuskegee Airmen never lost a bomber to enemy fire, and they received three Presidential Unit Citations. Their outstanding service contributed to the integration of America's armed forces by President Harry S Truman in 1948.

JT-20 MCCOY REVOLUTIONARY WAR SOLDIERS

On Sandy Point Road (Rte. 604) approximately 150 feet south of Cople Highway

(Rte. 202). Bennett and James McCoy, free men (probably brothers) from Westmoreland County, were among the many African Americans who served in the Virginia militia and the United States Army or Navy during the Revolutionary War. Bennett McCoy served for three years starting in 1777, participated in several major battles, and reenlisted with the 15th Virginia Regiment until the end of the war. James McCoy rendered guard service on the Potomac River from 1777 to 1778. In 1781, he was drafted and stationed on the York River at Yorktown and acted as a bowman to assist "his captain" in navigating the river. Each of the McCoys received a pension for his service.

JT-17   PRIVATE TATE—BUFFALO SOLDIER

On Zacata Road (Rte. 645) approximately two miles north of Kings Highway (Rte. 3). Walter Tate was born nearby in 1854. He enlisted as a private on 6 May 1879 at Fort Concho (present day San Angelo), Texas, in Company M, 10th Regiment, U.S. Cavalry. Tate and those who served with him on the western frontier defended settlements, livestock, the U.S. mail, and stage routes from bandits, cattle thieves, and Mexican revolutionaries. The Indians called Tate and other soldiers of color "Buffalo Soldiers" because of their dark curly hair, endurance, and strength, claiming that these attributes reminded them of their much-prized buffaloes. Tate was discharged on 5 May 1884. This buffalo soldier died in Westmoreland County in 1933.

JT-18   ZION BAPTIST CHURCH

On Cople Highway (Rte. 202) at intersection with Zion Church Road (Rte. 611). Zion Baptist Church is home to one of the oldest African American congregations in Westmoreland County. Before slavery ended, according to local tradition, services were first held under a dogwood bush arbor on Gawen's Farm, near Tucker Hill, approximately one and a half miles north of here. The members had most likely worshiped at the nearby white Machodoc (Sandy Valley) Baptist Church. Zion Baptist Church was formally organized in 1867, when the congregation constructed a log building. During the latter half of the 1800s, a fire and expanding membership required the construction of two other buildings. The present church was erected in 1932.

Headquarters building of Fort Concho, Texas. Marker JT-17. (Creative Commons)

Portrait of John Kirby (left) and Buster Bailey at the Brown Derby, Washington, D.C., c. May 1946. Photo by William P. Gottlieb. Library of Congress.

REGION TWO

Northern Piedmont, Valley, and Western Mountains

Augusta County

Bath County

Clarke County

Culpeper County

Fauquier County

City of Harrisonburg

City of Lexington

Madison County

Orange County

Rappahannock County

Rockbridge County

Rockingham County

Shenandoah County

City of Staunton

Warren County

City of Waynesboro

City of Winchester

AUGUSTA COUNTY

W-231 Augusta County Training School

On Cedar Green Road (Rte. 693) approximately 1000 feet east of William Cousins Road.   A rural African-American school stood here by 1874. In 1927 a two-room elementary school serving the Cedar Green and Smokey Row communities was built. The Augusta County Training School (Cedar Green School), the county's first black consolidated school, opened here in 1938. Community members assisted to construct this frame structure, featuring a central auditorium, a common design provided by the Virginia Department of Education. Between 250 to 320 students, grades one through nine, attended class here from across the county. Augusta County school integration in 1966 closed the school and the American Legion purchased the building.

BATH COUNTY

Q-36 T. C. Walker School

On Mountain Valley Road (Rte. 39) approximately 400 feet west of T. C. Walker Road. T. C. Walker School, which opened in 1930, was named for Thomas Calhoun Walker a former slave from Gloucester County who became the first African American attorney in Virginia. It cost $4,600, and was underwritten with $500 from the Julius Rosenwald Foundation, $505 from the local African American community, and $3,595 from the county. Virginia Turner was one of the longest serving teachers at the school, which had two classrooms, a kitchen, and library and remained open until 1965. This Rosenwald School was one of more than 5,000 built in 15 states between 1917 and 1932 to teach African American children.

D-38 The Rev. Dr. William H. Sheppard   (28 May 1865-25 Nov. 1927)

On Sam Snead Highway (Rte. 220) near the intersection with Mountain Valley Road (Rte. 39).   Born in Waynesboro to former slaves, William H. Sheppard became a Presbyterian missionary to the Belgian colony of Congo Free State in 1890. He and others opposed King Leopold II of Belgium, who encouraged such atrocities as the amputation of children's hands to intimidate Congolese rubber workers. On 21 Aug. 1904, while visiting his mother here, Sheppard spoke out at Warm Springs Presbyterian Church; reportedly, the Belgian ambassador attended. Later, in Africa, Sheppard published his charges, and the Belgian rubber monopoly sued for libel. After a judge dismissed the suit in Sept. 1909, an investigation verified Sheppard's claims and compelled improvements. Sheppard returned permanently to America in 1910.

Q-37 Union Hurst School

On Main Street (Rte. 615) approximately 300 feet east of Pinehurst Heights Road.   Union Hurst, a school for African Americans, was built near here on Pine Hurst Heights Road between 1924 and 1925. The school was built with the assistance of the Julius Rosenwald Fund, a program that helped build some 5,000 schools for African Americans in 15 states. Bath County and the African American community also contributed money for its construction. Teachers at the school included Booker T. Poteat and Nellie L. Perry. A high school room was added in 1932. In 1945, the high school portion was closed and students were bused to Covington in Alleghany County. The school closed in 1965.

CLARKE COUNTY

J-19 JOSEPHINE CITY

In Berryville at Josephine Street approximately 50 feet east of Church Street.
Early in the 1870s African Americans established Josephine City, a community originally composed of 31 one-acre lots lining a 16-foot wide street. Twenty-four former slaves and free blacks purchased the lots for $100 an acre from Ellen Mc-Cormick, owner of Clermont farm. The street and the community were probably named after a former slave at Clermont, Josephine Williams, purchaser of two lots. By 1900, Josephine City had become an oasis for the county's African Americans and was a self-sufficient community with a school, grocery store, gas station, boarding house, restaurant, cemetery, churches, and numerous residences.

J-43 LUCY DIGGS SLOWE
(4 JUL. 1883–21 OCT. 1937)

In Berryville on Josephine Street approximately 1000 feet east of Station Road.
Lucy Slowe, educator, was born in Berryville. In 1908, while attending Howard University, she became a founding member of Alpha Kappa Alpha Sorority, the first Greek letter organization for African American women, and was elected its first president. In 1917 Slowe won the national championship in women's singles at the segregated American Tennis Association's inaugural tournament. During her career as a public school teacher and principal, president of the National Association of College Women, English professor at Howard University, and Howard's first Dean of Women (1922-1937), Slowe worked to combat gender inequities and to prepare African American women for leadership.

CULPEPER COUNTY

J-97 ECKINGTON SCHOOL

Mount Pony Road (Rte. 658) approximately 180 feet west of Blackjack Road. The Eckington School was built in 1895 as a frame, one-room school for African American students from the nearby communities of Eckington and Poplar Ridge. The school building is typical of the ungraded schools of the 19th century that had all grades housed together in the same room. Such schools were common in rural communities until the mid-20th century. The Eckington School building closed in 1941. This structure stands as a rare example of the nearly vanished one-room schoolhouse type, illustrating the importance of education among the rural black community in the decades after the Civil War.

J-5 GEORGE WASHINGTON CARVER REGIONAL HIGH SCHOOL

At 9432 James Madison Highway (Rte. 15). George Washington Carver Regional High School was founded in 1948 to serve the educational needs of black students in Culpeper, Madison, Orange, and Rappahannock counties. Secondary schools for blacks in those counties were either nonexistent or inadequate for collegiate preparation. The regional high school was established as an economical solution to these problems. In 1968 the school was renamed the Piedmont Technical Education Center.

C-62 PETE HILL   (1882-1951)

On Rapidan Road (Rte. 615) approximately 250 feet south of Wilhoite Lane. John Preston "Pete" Hill, Negro League baseball player and manager, was born nearby on 12 Oct., probably 1882, and likely to formerly enslaved parents. Banned from whites-only major leagues, Hill became a star outfielder for African American teams, notably the Philadelphia Giants

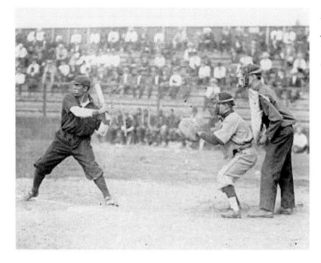

J. Preston "Pete" Hill at bat for the Leland Giants baseball team in Chicago, Illinois. Marker C-62 (Library of Congress)

and Chicago American Giants. A Cuban League 1910/11 winter-season batting champion (with a .365 average), Hill hit 28 home runs for the Detroit Stars in 1919 (when Babe Ruth hit 29 in more games), marking Hill as among black baseball's earliest power hitters. Hill died 19 Dec. 1951 and was inducted into the National Baseball Hall of Fame in 2006.

FAUQUIER COUNTY

FF-11 NUMBER 18 SCHOOL

On John Marshall Highway (Rte. 55) at intersection with Whiting Road.   After the Civil War, the constitution of 1869 established a statewide system of free public schools in Virginia. Several new schools in Fauquier were identified by an assigned number; Number 18 was built on land donated by Samuel F. Shackleford. From the time of its construction in 1887 until 1910, this one-room schoolhouse served local white children. When they moved to a newer school in the nearby village of Marshall in 1910, Number 18 then served African American students until it closed in 1964. Number 18 stands today as a rare example of a once-common schoolhouse.

CITY OF HARRISONBURG

A-120 EDGAR AMOS LOVE   (1891-1974)

At 455 Sterling Street.   Edgar Amos Love, son of a Methodist minister, was born in Harrisonburg in 1891. On 17 Nov. 1911, while a student at Howard University, he co-founded Omega Psi Phi, the first fraternity established at a historically black college. The organization later expanded beyond the United States. Ordained a minister in the Methodist Episcopal Church, Love served overseas as an army chaplain during World War I. He became a bishop in 1952 and worked to desegregate the church. Dedicated to social justice, he advocated nonviolent protest against discrimination and helped lead the Southern Conference Educational Fund, an interracial civil rights organization.

A-124 NEWTOWN CEMETERY

On Hill Street at intersection with Kelly Street.   African Americans established the community of Newtown in this area after the Civil War. In 1869 five trustees purchased land here for a cemetery open to "all persons of color." By 1920 the cemetery had expanded three times to accommodate Harrisonburg's growing African American population. Among the nearly 1,000 burials, some unmarked, are Civil War-era United States Colored Troops and veterans of World War I, World War II, Korea, and Vietnam. Also interred here are Harrisonburg's first African American city council member and several noted educators, including Lucy F. Simms. The cemetery is listed on the National Register of Historic Places.

CITY OF LEXINGTON

I-24 JOHN CHAVIS

On W. Washington Street approximately 200 feet west of Lee Avenue.   John Chavis (1763–1838), a free-born African-American veteran of the American Revolution was a native of Granville County, North Carolina. He was also one of the first college-educated men of color in the United States. Chavis studied at the College of New Jersey (now Princeton University) in 1792 and attended Liberty Hall Academy (present-day Washington and Lee University) by 1796. The Lexington Presbytery licensed him to preach in 1800. Chavis returned to North Carolina where he taught free blacks in the evenings and white students by day. One of the latter was Willie P. Mangum who became a U.S. Senator from North Carolina.

I-22-a ORIGINAL AFRICAN AMERICAN CEMETERY

On Lee Highway (Rte. 11) approximately 1500 feet north of Main Street.
Near the intersection of Washington and Lewis Streets stood the original burial ground for Lexington's substantial free black community and slaves dating to the early 1800s. The majority of the original burials were in unmarked graves and no records were maintained of these burials.

The Town of Lexington obtained ownership of the cemetery in 1876 and closed it in 1880 and the persons buried there were purportedly moved to Evergreen Cemetery, although there is little information to document the extent of the reburials. In 1946, the Town of Lexington subdivided the old cemetery and houses were built over the burial ground.

MADISON COUNTY

JE-8 CPL. CLINTON GREAVES (1855–1906)

In Madison at 2 S. Main Street (Rte. 231). Clinton Greaves (or Graves), Medal of Honor recipient, was born in Madison County, very likely into slavery. He enlisted in the U.S. Army in 1872 and served as a corporal in Co. C, 9th Cavalry. On 24 Jan. 1877 in the Florida Mountains of New Mexico, he was part of a small detachment sent to persuade about 50 Apache Indians to return to a reservation. The Apaches surrounded the cavalrymen until, in hand-to-hand combat, Greaves created a gap through which his companions escaped. On 26 June 1879, Pres. Rutherford B. Hayes awarded him the Medal of Honor for "extraordinary heroism." A U.S. military base in the Republic of Korea was later named Camp Greaves in his honor.

G-13 OAK GROVE BAPTIST CHURCH

On Oak Park Road (Rte. 634) approximately 500 feet west of Lilliards Ford Road.
Joe Thoms, Sr., a slave harness-maker, founded Oak Grove Baptist Church during the Civil War at his nearby log cabin, which burned in 1869. The congregation then met here, on land owned by John J. Robinson, a white farmer, in a grove of oak they called the "bush arbor." In 1870, Joe Thoms, with Deacons

Ambrose Tolliver, Frank Walker, Ed Redd, John Williams, Charles Brock, Spot Mallory, and Ambrose Thoms, built a small frame church here. The third church replaced it in 1894, when Robinson donated the land. A great-great-grandson of Joe Thoms became pastor in 1982.

ORANGE COUNTY

JJ-34 Capt. Andrew Maples Jr., Tuskegee Airman

In Orange on S. Madison Road (Rte. 15) at E. Church Street.   Andrew Maples grew up in Orange and completed the Civilian Pilot Training Program at Hampton Institute in 1941. He graduated from the Advanced Flying School at the Tuskegee Army Air Field on 14 Jan. 1943, was commissioned a second lieutenant in the Army Air Corps, and deployed to Italy with the 301st Fighter Squadron. On 26 June 1944, Maples's plane went down over the Adriatic Sea during a bomber escort mission. While officially missing in action, he was promoted to captain and awarded the Air Medal. The Army declared him dead in June 1945 and posthumously awarded him the Purple Heart. His name appears on the Tablets of the Missing at the Florence American Cemetery and Memorial in Italy.

JJ-26 Gilmore Farm

On Constitution Highway (Rte. 20) approximately 300 feet west of entrance to Montpelier.   George Gilmore was born into slavery at Montpelier about 1810. Like millions of African Americans throughout the South, Gilmore made the transition to freedom after the Civil War. Many emancipated slaves worked on the same plantations where they once labored. Gilmore, his wife Polly and five children lived in this cabin built by family members in 1873 and farmed the surrounding

fields. In 1901 George Gilmore obtained the deed for 16 acres from Dr. James A. Madison. After Gilmore's death in 1905 the property remained in the family until 1920. Archaeological and architectural investigations have resulted in the restoration of this rare example of a surviving freed family's cabin.

JJ-33 Isabella Lightfoot Training School

On Marquis Road (Rte. 669) at intersection with Independence Road (Rte. 650).   Isabella Miller Lightfoot, born in Pennsylvania and educated at Hampton Normal and Agricultural Institute, taught African American children in Orange County from the 1880s to the 1930s. With other African American patrons, she donated funds for a school built here in 1930, named in her honor. The building, later enlarged, served students through grade 11 until George Washington Carver Regional High School opened in 1948. Operating as an elementary school in subsequent years, the building burned in 1953. That year the county constructed a new brick Lightfoot Elementary School on Rte. 522 for African Americans. County schools were desegregated in 1967-68.

JJ-31 Orange Graded School — Rosenwald Funded

In Orange on Dailey Drive approximately 2500 feet west of Caroline Street (Rte. 15).   Orange Graded School, built in 1925 to replace the African American schoolhouse on West Main Street, stood here. Of the several county schools for black students, Orange Graded was the only one built using the Julius Rosenwald Fund, which was established in 1917 by the president of Sears, Roebuck and Company to construct schools for African Americans across the rural South. Of the $6,200 building cost, 40 percent was raised by the local African American community. This four-teacher standard plan school was one of the larger Rosenwalds built in Virginia. Gussie Baylor Taylor was recruited to teach in 1925 and later served as the school's supervisor.

JJ-32   SHADY GROVE SCHOOL

On Piney Woods Road (Rte. 667) approximately 1500 feet east of Monrovia Road (Rte. 612).   The Orange County School Board acquired five acres here in 1894 and established Shady Grove School for African American students. With contributions from African American patrons, the county erected a new two-room frame building here ca. 1923. Although the school received no money from the Julius Rosenwald Fund, its design reflected the architectural influence of that program, which helped construct thousands of schools for African Americans across the rural South. Shady Grove, which served grades 1-7, closed in 1954 when the brick Lightfoot Elementary School opened six miles northeast. The frame building was restored in 2007. Orange County schools were desegregated in 1967-68.

RAPPAHANNOCK COUNTY

J-101   JOHN JACKSON – TRADITIONAL MUSICIAN

On Sperryville Pike (Rte. 522), 1200 feet south of intersection with Hawlin Road.   John Jackson, Piedmont guitar master and influential traditional musician, was born near here on 25 Feb. 1924. One of fourteen children of tenant farmers Suddy and Hattie Jackson, Jackson learned songs on the guitar and banjo from his parents, traveling and local musicians, and records. He moved to Fairfax County in 1950, where he worked various jobs and started a grave-digging business. Introduced to the Washington, D.C., folk scene in 1964, Jackson performed on eight records, at clubs, on radio, and at festivals in the U.S. and Europe. He received the prestigious National Heritage Fellowship Award in 1986. Jackson died at home in Fairfax Station on 20 Jan. 2002.

C-35   WASHINGTON GRADED SCHOOL

In Washington at 267 Piedmont Avenue. Washington Graded School was built here ca. 1924 to serve African American students. The Parents' Civic League, a

National Heritage Fellowship portrait of John Jackson, by Tom Pich. Marker J-101. (National Endowment for the Arts)

local organization of African Americans, conveyed the land to the district school board. Contributions for the two-teacher building came from the black community ($1,200), Rappahannock County ($1,600), and the Julius Rosenwald Fund ($700). This fund, established by the president of Sears, Roebuck, and Co., and inspired by the work of Booker T. Washington, helped build more than 5,000 schools for black students between 1917 and 1932. Washington Graded School closed in 1967 when county schools were desegregated. The school is listed on the National Register of Historic Places.

ROCKBRIDGE COUNTY

L-63 FRANK PADGET WATER TRAGEDY

In Glasgow on Blue Ridge Road (Rte. 684) between McColluch and Anderson Streets. Heavy rains in late Jan. 1854 left the James River and the treacherous Balcony Falls in full flood. On 21 Jan., the canal boat *Clinton* and its passengers became stranded in the raging waters. Frank Padget, a skilled boatman and slave, led four other men to rescue them. In a heroic attempt to save the last passenger, Padget drowned, unable to fight the rushing current. Capt. Edward Echols, who witnessed Padget's act, was so moved he commissioned the construction of a granite obelisk monument that was erected beside Lock 16 of the Blue Ridge Canal. It now stands here in Glasgow's Centennial Park.

A-51 VIRGINIA INVENTORS

On W. Lee Highway (Rte. 11) at intersection with Raphine Road (Rte. 606). At Walnut Grove farm, about a mile northwest of here, Cyrus H. McCormick and Jo Anderson, an enslaved African American, developed a mechanical grain reaper by 1831. McCormick later built a factory in Chicago and, using innovative marketing techniques, far outsold other manufacturers. The reaper revolutionized agricultural efficiency. James E. A. Gibbs, who patented a number of improvements to the sewing machine, was born near here in 1829. His company, Willcox and Gibbs, became a leading producer of commercial sewing machines late in the 19th century.

ROCKINGHAM COUNTY

D-1-a LONG'S CHAPEL AND ZENDA

At 1334-B Fridleys Gap Road.   Long's Chapel was built in 1870, a year after William and Hannah Carpenter and the Church of the United Brethren in Christ deeded land here "to colored people . . . for . . . a church, burial ground, and a school house." Henry Carter, Milton Grant, William Timbers, and Richard Fortune, all formerly enslaved, owned two-acre "home plots" where the community of Zenda grew to 17 households of 80 people by 1900. The school, where notable Harrisonburg educator Lucy Simms began her career, closed in 1925. In Zenda, blacks freely exercised new rights to worship, marriage, education, property, and burial in a marked gravesite.

D-44 NEWTOWN (EAST ELKTON) SCHOOL

In Newtown on Newtown Road (Rte. 759) just west of Samuels Road.   The Newtown School, built here in 1921-1922, served African American students during the segregation era. Julius Rosenwald, president of Sears, Roebuck, and Co., collaborated with Booker T. Washington in a school-building campaign beginning in 1912. The Rosenwald Fund, incorporated in 1917, helped build more than 5,000 schools and supporting structures for African Americans in the rural South by 1932. The Fund contributed $1,000 toward the Newtown School, while

James River canal boats depicted in 1865 Harper's Weekly. *Marker L-63. (Library of Congress)*

local African Americans donated $872 and Rockingham County gave $2,628. The three-teacher school, the county's last solely for black students, closed in 1965 and is the only remaining Rosenwald-funded school building in the county.

SHENANDOAH COUNTY

A-126   Mt. Zion Methodist Church

In Woodstock at 158 N. Church Street. Inspired by visits from traveling preachers, African Americans in Woodstock organized what would become Mt. Zion United Methodist Church ca. 1867. The congregation acquired the framework of a former German Reformed church in 1869, moved it to this site, and used it to construct a sanctuary. In a town segregated by race, this church was the center of the African American neighborhood and hosted religious, educational, political, and social events. After black residents campaigned for a school building, Woodstock's first African American public school was built on the church lot in 1882. The congregation constructed a new sanctuary here in 1921 under the leadership of the Rev. W. H. Polk.

CITY OF STAUNTON

I-32   Montgomery Hall Park

At 1000 Montgomery Avenue. Montgomery Hall Park, a municipal park for African Americans during the segregation era, opened on 4 July 1947. The Rev. T. J. Jemison of Mt. Zion Baptist Church, an African American community leader, persuaded Staunton City Council to purchase about 150 acres for the project. The land had been part of John Howe Peyton's Montgomery Hall plantation, established early in the 19th century. A committee of African American citizens appointed by City Council managed the park, which featured a swimming pool, bowling alley, and picnic facilities and drew crowds from throughout central Virginia. Staunton's park system was desegregated late in the 1960s.

Picnic at Montgomery Hall Park. Marker I-32. (Augusta County Historical Society)

WARREN COUNTY

J-22 Warren County High School and Massive Resistance

In Front Royal on Luray Avenue at Oakridge Court.   Warren County High School, a Public Works Administration project, was constructed in 1940. In 1958, the local NAACP chapter, led by James W. Kilby, won a federal suit against the Warren County School Board to admit African Americans for the first time. In response, Gov. James Lindsay Almond Jr. ordered it closed in Sept. 1958, the first school in Virginia shut down under the state's Massive Resistance strategy. Following the 1959 Virginia Supreme Court of Appeals ruling that Massive Resistance was unconstitutional, a U.S. Circuit Court ordered it reopened. On 18 Feb. 1959, 23 African American students walked up this hill and integrated the school.

CITY OF WAYNESBORO

Q-2 Port Republic Road Historic District

On Port Republic Road at Fontaine Street.   This is Waynesboro's oldest intact neighborhood. It coalesced as a community about 1870, just after the Civil War, when formerly enslaved individuals moved here to work in nearby industries and on railroads. The African American residents constructed most of the buildings here between the mid-19th and mid-20th centuries. The community's Rosenwald School and Shiloh Baptist Church were both constructed in 1924. One of the earliest houses in the district, a circa 1818 dwelling, was built on Riverside Drive. Designated the Port Republic Road Historic District, the neighborhood was listed on the National Register of Historic Places in 2002.

CITY OF WINCHESTER

Q-4-j   JOHN KIRBY, JAZZ MUSICIAN

On N. Kent Street between Kern and Elk Streets.   Born on 31 Dec. 1908, John Kirk (John Kirby) was raised here by the Rev. Washington Johnson. He learned to play the piano and trombone and then moved to Baltimore in the 1920s where he picked up the tuba and bass. In New York City by 1930, he played bass in legendary bands led by Chick Webb and Fletcher Henderson. In 1937, the John Kirby Sextet was formed at the Onyx Club on West 52d Street in New York City. Billed as "The Biggest Little Band in the Land," they were known for their musical precision and intricate arrangements and performed nationally into the middle 1940s. Kirby died on 14 June 1952 in Hollywood, California.

Historic homes in the Port Republic Road Historic District. Marker Q-2. (DHR-136-5054)

Reverend John Jasper was renowned for his fiery oratorical style and for the sermon, "De Sun Do Move," first delivered in 1878. (New York Public Library Digital Collections)

REGION THREE

Central Virginia and Central Piedmont

Albemarle County

Amelia County

Caroline County

City of Charlottesville

Chesterfield County

Dinwiddie County

Fluvanna County

City of Fredericksburg

Goochland County

Hanover County

Henrico County

Louisa County

City of Petersburg

Powhatan County

City of Richmond

Spotsylvania County

ALBEMARLE COUNTY

G-5   FREE STATE

On Belvedere Boulevard near Free State Road.   Free State, a community of free African Americans, stood here. Its nucleus was a 224-acre tract that Amy Farrow, a free black woman, purchased in 1788. Her son Zachariah Bowles lived here and married Critta Hemings of Monticello, an older sister of Sally Hemings. Free State residents farmed and practiced trades, accumulated personal property, and did business with local whites. The small community expanded after the Civil War and by early in the 20th century was home to the Free State Colored School and the Central Relief Association, a local benevolent society.

G-22   PROFFIT HISTORIC DISTRICT

On Mossing Ford Road (Rte. 741) at Proffit Road (Rte. 649).   Ben Brown and other newly freed slaves, who founded the community after the Civil War, first named the settlement Egypt and then Bethel. About 1881, the community became known as Proffit when the Virginia Midland Railway placed a stop here, stimulating further development between 1890 and 1916 by white landowners who built along Proffit Road. Prominent reminders of Proffit's black heritage are Evergreen Baptist Church, built in 1891, and several houses constructed by the Brown and Flannagan families in the 1880s. The district was listed on the Virginia Landmarks Register in 1998 and the National Register of Historic Places in 1999.

GA-48   ST. JOHN SCHOOL—ROSENWALD FUNDED

At 1595 St. John Road.   The St. John School, built here in 1922-1923, served African American students during the segregation era. Julius Rosenwald, president of Sears, Roebuck and Co., collaborated with Booker T. Washington in a school-building campaign beginning in 1912. The Rosenwald Fund, incorporated in 1917, helped build more than 5,000 schools and supporting structures for African Americans in the rural South by 1932. The Rosenwald Fund contributed $700 for the St. John School, while local residents donated $500 and Albemarle County provided $1,300. The two-classroom school closed during the 1950s and was later purchased by St. John Baptist Church.

AMELIA COUNTY

OL-12   McDowell Delaney (1844–1926)

On Pridesville Road (Rte. 681) about 1000 feet east of Eggleston Road (Rte. 630). McDowell Delaney was born to free African American parents in Amelia County. During the Civil War he worked as a cook and teamster for the 14th Virginia Infantry Regiment. He later attended a school taught by his father and managed property at the Freedmen's Bureau Hospital in Farmville. Delaney represented Amelia in the Virginia House of Delegates from 1871 to 1873 and participated in a state convention of African Americans in 1875. He served the county as a justice of the peace, constable, and coroner. Delaney, an ordained minister, was pastor of Chester Grove Baptist Church for 35 years.

CAROLINE COUNTY

E- 115   GABRIEL'S REBELLION

On Richmond Turnpike (Rte. 301), 500 feet north of Pamunkey River bridge.   On 24 Aug. 1800, slave Ben Woolfolk met with other slaves at nearby Littlepage's Bridge to recruit individuals for an insurrection planned for 30 Aug. The insurgents led by Gabriel, a slave owned by Thomas Henry

John Cephas (right) and Phil Wiggins. Marker E-230. (Elvert Xavier Barnes Photography)

Prosser of Henrico County, intended to march into Richmond, capture Governor James Monroe, and force him and other leaders to support political, social, and economic equality. Intense rains delayed the scheme. Mosby Sheppard of Henrico County notified Monroe of the conspiracy after his slaves, Tom and Pharoah, made him aware of the plot. Monroe called out the militia, who captured many of the alleged conspirators. Trials were held in a number of jurisdictions, including Caroline County, resulting in the execution of Gabriel and at least 25 supporters.

E-230 JOHN CEPHAS (1930–2009)

In Bowling Green at 268 N. Main Street. Born in Washington D.C., John Cephas grew up there and in Caroline County. He was influenced at an early age by his mother's singing, and a cousin taught him the highly syncopated and danceable guitar style now known as Piedmont Blues, which employs a complex, fin-ger-picking approach. Cephas performed at rural dance parties and as a gospel singer, developing his rich voice. He, and harmonica master Phil Wiggins, made numerous awarding-winning albums and performed all over the world, earning the W. C. Handy Award as Blues Entertainers of the Year in 1987. Cephas received the coveted National Heritage Fellowship from the National Endowment for the Arts in 1989.

ND-16 RICHARD AND MILDRED LOVING

On Richmond Turnpike (Rte. 301) just north of intersection with Sparta Road (Rte. 721). Richard Loving and Mildred Jeter, of different racial backgrounds, grew up near Central Point, 11 miles east of here. They fell in love and in June 1958 were married in Washington, D.C. After returning to Central Point, they were arrested for violating the state's laws against interracial marriage, which made it a felony for interracial couples to leave Virginia, marry, and resume residence in the state. The Lovings were convicted in 1959 at the Caroline County courthouse. The case reached the Virginia Supreme Court of Appeals, which in 1966 upheld the state's laws. In 1967 the U.S. Supreme Court's landmark ruling in *Loving v. Virginia* overturned all laws prohibiting interracial marriage.

Charles B. Holt House.
Marker Q-28-a.
(DHR 104-5098)

E-99-a YORK: LEWIS AND CLARK
EXPEDITION

On Jefferson Davis Highway (Rte. 1) ap-
proximately 1000 feet north of Ladysmith
Road. Born in Caroline County in 1770,
York was a slave of the William Clark
family and the only African American on
the 1803-1806 Lewis and Clark Expedition. Approximately 34 years old at the
time, York was one of the hunters and
also accompanied groups of soldiers on
scouting missions. Other members of the
expedition received money and land for
their services, but York did not because
of his slave status and Clark's refusal to
manumit him. York may have escaped
from Clark and returned to Wyoming,
where according to tradition, he lived out
his life with the Crow Indians.

CITY OF CHARLOTTESVILLE

Q-28-a C. B. HOLT ROCK HOUSE

At 1010 Preston Avenue. African American Charles B. Holt owned a carpentry
business in Charlottesville's Vinegar Hill
neighborhood. The son of former slaves,
Holt built this Arts and Crafts–style
house in 1925–1926, during the era of

segregation when blacks were more than
a quarter of the city's population but
owned less than one-tenth of its private
land. He lived here with his wife, Mary
Spinner, until his death in 1950. Later
Holt's stepson, Roy C. Preston, and his
wife, Asalie Minor Preston, moved in.
After a distinguished career teaching
in Albemarle County's segregated black
public schools, Asalie Preston endowed
the Minor-Preston Educational Fund to
provide college scholarships.

Q-16 FIRST BAPTIST CHURCH

At 632 W. Main Street. The Charlottesville African Church congregation was organized in 1864. Four years later it bought
the Delevan building, built in 1828 by
Gen. John H. Cocke, and at one time used
as a temperance hotel for University of Virginia students. It became part of the Charlottesville General Hospital and sheltered
wounded soldiers during the Civil War.
The church members laid the cornerstone
for a new building in 1877 on the Delevan
site, and the First Baptist Church, West
Main Street, was completed in 1883. This
building is listed on the National Register
of Historic Places.

Q-30 Jefferson School

On 4th Street NW at Commerce Street.
The name Jefferson School has a long
association with African American
education in Charlottesville. It was first
used in the 1860s in a Freedmen's Bureau
school and then for a public grade school
by 1894. Jefferson High School opened
here in 1926 as the city's first high school
for blacks, an early accredited black high
school in Virginia. The facility became
Jefferson Elementary School in 1951. In
1958, some current and former Jefferson
students requested transfers to two white
schools. The state closed the two white
schools. Their reopening in 1959 began
the process of desegregation in Charlottesville. Jefferson School housed many
different educational programs after
integrating in 1965.

CHESTERFIELD COUNTY

K-338 Amaza Lee Meredith
(1895–1984)

*On the campus of Virginia State Univer-
sity about 500 feet south of Matthews
Jefferson Drive.*   Lynchburg native
Amaza Lee Meredith was one of the
nation's few African American female
architects during the mid-20th century.
Her self-designed residence, Azurest
South (1939), is a rare Virginia example
of a mature International Style building. She also designed houses in New
York, Texas, and elsewhere in Virginia.
Principally employed as a teacher, Meredith founded the fine arts department
at present-day Virginia State University
and served as chair until her retirement
in 1958. She willed her half of Azurest
South to the university alumni association after her death. It was listed on
the Virginia Landmarks Register and
National Register of Historic Places in
1993.

S-89 First Baptist Church
(Centralia)

*On Centralia Road (Rte. 145) at Centralia
Station.* In 1867, the African American
members of nearby Salem Baptist Church
separated and founded Salem African
Baptist Church. The new congregation
held worship services under a brush
arbor before constructing a building here
on a one-acre tract deeded in 1869 by
members of the mother church. The congregation soon changed its name to First
Baptist Church (Centralia). Early in the
20th century, members erected a large
new sanctuary incorporating elements of
the Gothic Revival and Colonial Revival

*Azurest South, the
residence of Amaza
Lee Meredith.
Marker K-338.
(DHR 104-5098)*

styles. Razed by fire in 1996, this structure was rebuilt to original specifications in 1997. In 1963, the growing congregation moved two miles east.

S-97   George Washington Carver High School

Near 12400 Branders Bridge Road. After African American patrons campaigned for a new high school, the Chesterfield County School Board opened the consolidated George Washington Carver High School here in 1948. Carver, which replaced the old Hickory Hill and Daniel Webster Davis High Schools, was for 22 years the county's only public high school for black students. William A. Brown, Carver's sole principal, led a dedicated faculty and staff. The building, which also housed offices for school administrators and agricultural and home economics demonstration agents, was a literary and cultural center for the African American community. Carver closed in 1970, when the county finished implementing its desegregation plan.

O-75   Midlothian Elementary School

Near 13801 Westfield Road. First African Baptist Church of Coalfield, which stood about a mile southeast of here, opened a school for African Americans in 1866. After a fire in 1877, the congregation moved here and renamed itself First Baptist Church of Midlothian. Church trustees conveyed land to the local school board for the construction of Midlothian Elementary School on this site. The first frame schoolhouse was replaced in 1925-1926 with the assistance of the Julius Rosenwald Fund, which helped build more than 5,000 schools and supporting structures for black students between 1917 and 1932. The school occupied

a new brick building here in 1948; it closed in 1969 as Chesterfield County desegregated its schools.

K-324   Virginia State University

In Ettrick on E. River Road 100 feet west of Matthews Jefferson Drive. The Virginia Normal and Collegiate Institute was chartered on 6 Mar. 1882. The Readjuster Party was instrumental in supporting a state institution of higher education in Virginia for African Americans with some unusual features to the charter on the institute. It called for six of the seven members of the board of visitors be black, an all-black faculty, as well as the authority to grant college degrees. This is in contrast to many African American agricultural and industrial schools established at that time. Classes began in October 1883 with 62 students, six faculty members, and one building. In 1920 land grant status was acquired and the current name was conferred in 1979.

DINWIDDIE COUNTY

I-6   Central State Hospital

On Washington Street (Rte. 1) at 7th Avenue. Central State Hospital traces its origins to a mental health hospital for African Americans established ca. 1866 by the Freedmen's Bureau at Howard's Grove, near Richmond. The Commonwealth of Virginia assumed control of the facility in 1870. In 1882 the City of Petersburg purchased the Mayfield plantation here for $15,000 and transferred the property to the hospital's board of directors. The hospital relocated in 1885 on completion of the new physical plant, which continued to expand during the 20th century. The facility provided mental health care to nonwhite Virginians until it was desegregated in the mid-1960s.

Elizabeth Hobbs Keckley. Marker S-85. (Library of Virginia)

S-95 DINWIDDIE NORMAL INDUSTRIAL SCHOOL (SOUTHSIDE HIGH SCHOOL)

At 12318 Boydton Plank Road (Rte. 1). Dinwiddie Normal Industrial School, the first African American high school built in the county during the segregation era, stood three miles southeast. When the building burned in 1953, plans were already in progress to construct a modern facility on this site as part of county efforts to build "separate but equal" schools. Bids came from across the region, and in Aug. 1952, the school board chose Farmville's Mottley Construction Co. to build the new school, which was renamed Southside High School. The school opened in spring 1954 with 520 students. Dr. Roy Watson served as principal. The school was closed in 2012.

S-85 ELIZABETH HOBBS KECKLEY (1818–1907)

On Boydton Plank Road (Rte. 1) about 200 feet north of Sappony Creek. Born near here in Dinwiddie County in 1818, Elizabeth Hobbs Keckley (sometimes Keckly) was a dressmaker and abolitionist. She lived as a slave in Virginia and North Carolina but eventually bought her freedom in 1855. By 1860 she had relocated to Baltimore and then to Washington, D.C. Because of her dressmaking skills, she became the seamstress, personal maid, and confidante to Mary Todd Lincoln, President Abraham Lincoln's wife. In 1868, Keckley's account, *Behind the Scenes; or, Thirty Years a Slave and Four Years in the White House*, appeared and met with criticism from Mrs. Lincoln for its candor. Keckley died in 1907.

FLUVANNA COUNTY

F-99 JOHN JASPER

On James Madison Highway (Rte. 15) at Carysbrook Road. The Rev. John Jasper, one of the best known black preachers of the 19th century in Virginia, was born a slave in Fluvanna County on 4 July 1812. After working in a tobacco factory, Jasper had a religious awakening in the later 1830s and became a preacher. Self-educated, Jasper was renowned for his fiery oratorical style and for the sermon, "De Sun Do Move," first delivered in 1878 and preached to more than 250 audiences, including the Virginia General Assembly. He organized the Sixth Mount Zion Baptist Church in Richmond in 1867. Jasper died in late March 1901 and is buried in Richmond.

F-48 S. C. ABRAMS HIGH SCHOOL

On James Madison Highway (Rte. 15) about 100 feet north of Central Plains Road. Fluvanna County dedicated its only African American high school on 21 Nov. 1936 and named it the S. C. Abrams High School to honor the Rev. Samuel Christopher Abrams, who served as the county supervisor for the black schools and also as a minister in several Baptist churches. Before 1934 black students had to leave the county to attend high school, but in 1934 a temporary high school opened in a wood-frame building adjacent to New Fork Baptist Church. By 1936 money raised by the black community and the county provided black students with Abrams High School, which became a junior high following the integration of the schools in the 1960s. The Abrams building, located one mile west, has housed administrative offices since 1991.

CITY OF FREDERICKSBURG

N-33   FREDERICKSBURG NORMAL AND INDUSTRIAL INSTITUTE

On Tyler Street between Dixon (Rte. 17) and White Streets.   Due to the efforts of local blacks, the Fredericksburg Normal and Industrial Institute (FNII) opened in October 1905 at the Shiloh New Site Baptist Church with about 20 students. In 1906 the board of trustees purchased land and a large farmhouse here, named it Mayfield, and opened the school in the autumn. The course of study, modeled after a university curriculum included teacher education classes as well as English, mathematics, history, geography, literature, Greek, and music. By 1938, Mayfield High School had become a part of the segregated city school system.

GOOCHLAND COUNTY

SA-27   DAHLGREN'S CAVALRY RAID

On River Road (Rte. 650) between River-gate Drive and Hill Point Road.
In February 1864 a young Union officer, Col. Ulric Dahlgren, joined with Brig. Gen. H. Judson Kilpatrick to raid Richmond and free Federal prisoners of war. They planned for Kilpatrick's men to

attack the city's northern defenses while Dahlgren would lead his men through Goochland County, cross the James River, and enter the city from the south. A local African American, Martin Robinson escorted the troopers to a nearby ford but the water was too high to cross. Suspecting trickery, Dahlgren hanged him near here on 1 March, and then attacked the city from the west. Defeated, he rode east in search of Kilpatrick and was killed the next day in King and Queen County.

SA-59   FIRST BAPTIST CHURCH, MANAKIN

At 224 River Road West (Rte. 6).   Organized as Dover Mines Church about 1863, First Baptist Church, Manakin is one of the oldest African American churches in Goochland County. Its members separated from Dover Baptist Church. Initially conducting their services at different sites, the Dover Mines congregation eventually converted a tool house into a church nearby. In 1891, trustees W. T. Taylor, Scott Houston, and John Christian purchased the Deitrick Hotel lot property here. Church members built this picturesque Italianate church in 1922, using some bricks from the 18th century. According to tradition, the church members hauled the 18th-century bricks from the nearby ruins of Dover Anglican Church.

SA-12   SECOND UNION SCHOOL

At 2843 Hadensville–Fife Road (Rte. 606). Second Union School, which operated until 1959 is the oldest-surviving of the 10 Rosenwald schools built in Goochland County. The African American community and Goochland County contributed funds to the building. Constructed in 1918, the building is a one-story, two-room, two-teacher-plan school with a brick interior chimney on the rear wall.

Original chalkboards survive in both rooms. The school is among 5,000 built using money and plans from the Julius Rosenwald Fund in 15 states including 367 in Virginia.

SA-70   THE 1936 VIRGINIA PRISON RECORDINGS

On River Road West (Rte. 6) approximately 125 west of State Farm Road. In 1936 famed folklorist John A. Lomax visited the Virginia State Prison Farm here and at the Virginia State Penitentiary in Richmond. Working for the Library of Congress's Archive of Folk Song, Lomax canvassed southern prisons in search of traditional African American music. On 13 and 14 June 1936, Lomax, assisted by Harold Spivacke, recorded quartets, banjo tunes, work songs, spirituals, and blues at the State Farm. Among the notable performers were inmates Jimmie Strother and Joe Lee. The Library of Congress first released songs from the sessions in the 1940s and they have appeared on many recordings since. These sessions are among the earliest aural records of Virginia's black folk-song tradition.

HANOVER COUNTY

I-10-C   CEDAR CREEK QUAKER MEETING HOUSE

On W. Patrick Henry Road (Rte. 54) at Quaker Church Road.   English immigrant Thomas Stanley, born about 1670, championed the right to religious freedom early in the 1700s. Stanley gave nearby land for a Quaker meetinghouse, school, and cemetery. Until the 19th century, the Religious Society of Friends (Quakers) convened here for worship. Here in 1767, Quakers spoke out strongly against enslavement of blacks, which resulted in a 1772 resolution prohibiting the purchase and hiring of slaves by Quakers.

By 1779, they had recommended freeing all slaves and approximately 200 were freed as a result. In 1875, the meeting was disbanded because of westward Quaker migration. The building burned in 1904.

ND-12   JANIE PORTER BARRETT
(9 AUG. 1865–27 AUG. 1948)

In Hanover on Hanover Courthouse Road (Rte. 301) approximately 400 feet south of Peaks and Georgetown Roads.   Janie Porter Barrett was born in Athens, Ga. She graduated from Hampton Institute and soon began teaching home-management techniques to other young African American women and girls. In 1915, Barrett founded the Industrial School for Wayward Colored Girls nearby, the third reform school specifically for black girls in the United States. The school long survived its predecessors in Maryland and Missouri, and was also the first--and for several years the only--such state-supported school. Barrett used progressive, humane methods, operating on an honor system and forbidding corporal punishment. In 1950, the school was renamed the Janie Porter School for Girls.

ND-13   JOHN HENRY SMYTH
(14 JULY 1844–5 SEPT. 1908)

On Hanover Courthouse Road (Rte. 301) approximately 500 feet north of River Road.   Born in Richmond, Va., to a free black mother and enslaved father, John Henry Smyth graduated from Howard University Law School in Washington, D.C., in 1872 and worked variously as a teacher, bank cashier, lawyer, and newspaper editor. He served as minister resident and consul general to Liberia, 1878-1885. His most enduring legacy, however, is the Hanover Juvenile Correctional Center, founded by him in 1897 as the Virginia Manual Labor School, among the first in the United States especially for African American youths. Smyth required his charges to labor on the school's farm to develop a strong work ethic. The center's school is named for him.

E-142   SCHOOL TRANSPORTATION

In Ashland on N. Washington Highway (Rte. 1) about 100 feet south of intersection with Berkley Street. Virginia public school boards began providing transportation to white students early in the 20th century but frequently denied this service to African Americans. Black children often had to walk miles to school, leading to non-attendance. Across Virginia in the 1930s, black community organizations raised funds for buses. Lucian Hunter, supported by the Chickahominy Baptist Association, acquired Hanover County's first school bus for African Americans ca. 1934. His sons Clarence, Earl, and Chester drove students to the Hanover County Training School. Petitioned by Hunter and others, the school board voted in 1935 to contribute funds toward this service. County schools were desegregated in 1969.

HENRICO COUNTY

V-26   BATTLE OF NEW MARKET HEIGHTS

On New Market Road (Rte. 5) approximately 100 feet west of New Market Heights Lane. On 28 September 1864, elements of Maj. Gen. Benjamin F. Butler's Army of the James crossed the James River to assault the Confederate defenses of Richmond. At dawn on 29 September, 6 regiments of U.S. Colored Troops fought with exceptional valor during their attack along New Market Road. Despite heavy casualties, they carried the earthworks there and succeeded in capturing New Market Heights, north of the road. Of the 20 Medals of Honor awarded to "Negro" soldiers and sailors during the Civil War, 14 were bestowed for this battle. Butler wrote that "the capacity of the negro race for soldiers had then and there been fully settled forever."

E-102   GABRIEL'S REBELLION

On Brook Road (Rte. 1) about 100 feet north of Upham Brook. Gabriel, a slave of Thomas Prosser of nearby Brookfield

The Butler Medal was the only medal created during the Civil War to honor a specific regiment or action, and the only medal ever struck for black troops. Major General Benjamin F. Butler funded the production of 197 silver and 11 bronze versions of this medal that were awarded to African American soldiers who served under his command at the Battle of New Market Heights. Markers EM-3, KV-32, Q-8-z, SA-41, V-26, W-94, and WY-11-a. (Tim Evanson, photographer, photograph May 15, 2012. Encyclopedia Virginia)

plantation, planned a slave insurrection against Richmond on 30 Aug. 1800. The slaves intended to kidnap Governor James Monroe and compel him to support political, social, and economic equality but intense rains delayed the insurgents' scheme. Mosby Sheppard, of Meadow Farm, informed of the plot by family slaves Tom and Pharaoh, dispatched a warning letter to the governor. Monroe called out the militia and Gabriel, his plans foiled, fled to Norfolk. Authorities there captured and returned him to Richmond. Convicted of conspiracy, Gabriel was hanged on 10 Oct. 1800, the last of twenty-six conspirators executed.

V-43   Pleasants v. Pleasants

On New Market Road (Rte. 5) approximately 350 feet east of Long Bridge Road. John Pleasants, Sr., nearby landowner and Quaker, requested in his will that his slaves be freed when each became 30 years old. Pleasants died in 1771, but it was not until 1782 that some of his slaves gained freedom when the Virginia General Assembly approved private manumissions. His son, Robert Pleasants, and a few other heirs freed close to 100 slaves in multiple counties. Robert Pleasants attempted to get all of the family to honor the will's stipulations, which culminated in 1798 when the Virginia High Court of Chancery heard it as a legal case. Future U.S. Chief Justice John Marshall and John Warden represented Robert Pleasants on behalf of the slaves. In 1799, the court ruled in favor of freeing the slaves. Some of the freed slaves settled nearby on Robert Pleasants's land to form the Gravely Hill community.

S-31-a   Tommy Edwards (1922–1969)

On Pemberton Road (Rte. 157) approximately 100 feet north of Quioccasin Road. Born Thomas Jefferson Edwards here in

Tommy Edwards' MGM publicity photo that appeared in Billboard *magazine on October 6, 1958. Marker S-31-a. (Creative Commons)*

Henrico County on 15 Oct. 1922, African American singer-songwriter Tommy Edwards composed songs recorded by well-known performers Tony Bennett, Red Foley, Tony Fontane, and Louis Jordan. He recorded for Top and National Records before joining MGM and scoring several hits, including "It's All in the Game," in 1951. In 1958 an updated version of the song sold more than 3,000,000 copies. He charted 13 more songs and released 12 albums before his death on 23 Oct. 1969. His fame is preserved by the enduring popularity of his signature song. Edwards is interred in nearby Quioccasin Baptist Church Cemetery.

W-221   Virginia Estelle Randolph

At 2200 Mountain Road.   The daughter of parents born in slavery, Virginia Randolph (1874-1958) taught in a one-room schoolhouse beginning in 1892. A gifted teacher, she became in 1908 the nation's first Jeanes Supervising Industrial Teacher, a position sponsored by the Anna T. Jeanes Fund of Philadelphia for black Southern education. Randolph developed the Henrico Plan, teaching both traditional subjects and vocational skills. Henrico County named two schools in her honor here in 1915 and 1957. In 1969 the schools were merged to form the Virginia Randolph Education Center; Randolph is buried here.

E-103   YOUNG'S SPRING

On Lakeside Avenue (Rte. 161) at Park Street. Just one block southwest at Young's Spring on Upham Brook, slaves often congregated on weekends to hold religious services and social gatherings. This is where Gabriel, a slave of William Prosser, planned the slave rebellion scheduled for 30 August 1800. Gabriel and his followers plotted to capture Richmond and to demand their freedom. The attack never took place because a turbulent thunderstorm made roads and bridges to the city impassable. Governor James Monroe, learning of the plot, mustered the militia. Eventually, most of the conspirators were captured and twenty-six slaves were executed.

LOUISA COUNTY

W-212-a   FLORA MOLTON
(1908–1990)

On Richmond Road (Rte. 250) at intersection with Zion Road (Rte. 627). Flora Molton sang what she called "spiritual and truth music," a combination of traditional religious songs and her own compositions. Born here in Louisa County, the daughter of the Reverend and Mrs. William Rollins, she began singing in church. At local parties she heard slide guitar played with a knife, a style she adopted to accompany herself. In 1937, she moved to Washington, D.C.,

to make her living playing music on the street, and was known and loved by the generations who encountered her there. She also performed at festivals and clubs, recorded three albums, and was featured in two documentary films.

W-235   HENRY BOX BROWN

On Jefferson Highway (Rte. 33) approximately 2000 feet east of Cross Country Road (Rte. 522). Born into slavery about 1815 at The Hermitage Plantation near here, Henry Brown was working in Richmond by 1830. Brown mailed himself to Philadelphia, and freedom, on 23 Mar. 1849 inside a three-foot-long box. Brown became a spokesperson for the abolitionist movement and symbol of the Underground Railroad. He published with Charles Stearns the *Narrative of Henry Box Brown* and exhibited a moving panorama, "The Mirror of Slavery." Forced to leave the country in Oct. 1850 after the Fugitive Slave Act because of the threat of re-enslavement, Brown moved to Great Britain where he toured as an entertainer. He returned to the United States in 1875 and died sometime after 1889.

W-222   JOHN MERCER LANGSTON BIRTHPLACE

In Louisa on W. Main Street (Rte. 33) at Courthouse Square. John Mercer Langston was born 5.5 miles N.W. of here on 14 Dec. 1829, son of plantation owner Ralph Quarles and his former slave Lucy Langston. A graduate of Oberlin College (1849), in 1855 Langston became township clerk of Brownhelm, Ohio—the first African American popularly elected to office. During the Civil War, he recruited regiments for the Union army. Afterward, he was founder and first dean of the Law Department of Howard University, served as minister resident in Haiti and *chargé d'affaires* in Santo Domingo, and was first president of what is now Virginia State University. In 1888 he became the first black congressman elected from Virginia. He died on 15 Nov. 1897 in Washington, D.C.

W-238   RICHARDSON AND MORTON SCHOOLS

At 1782 Jefferson Highway (Rte. 33). Louisa Training School, the county's first high school for African American students, was built three miles northwest in 1926 with aid from the Rosenwald Fund. In 1953, Archie Gibbs Richardson High School replaced it here as part of an effort to provide "separate but equal" facilities for African Americans. The school was named for the only black official then employed by Virginia's Education Department. Also on this site stood Zelda Carter Morton Elementary School, built in 1960 and named for the county's Jeanes Fund supervisor of education for blacks from 1926 to 1945. Louisa County schools were desegregated in 1969.

W-243   SHADY GROVE (ROSENWALD) SCHOOL

At 2924 Three Chopt Road (Rte. 634).

African Americans in this area organized a patrons' league and campaigned in the 1920s for a new school to replace the inadequate facility then in use. Shady Grove School, built on a standard one-teacher architectural plan, opened here in 1925 for students in grades 1-7. Funding for the building came from the African American community ($700), Louisa County ($400), and the Julius Rosenwald Fund ($400). The Rosenwald Fund, established by the president of Sears, Roebuck, and Co. and inspired by the work of Booker T. Washington, helped build more than 5,000 schools and supporting structures for African Americans in the rural South between 1917 and 1932. Shady Grove School closed in 1962.

CITY OF PETERSBURG

QA-31   BISHOP PAYNE DIVINITY SCHOOL

At 228 Halifax Street.   The Bishop Payne Divinity School began here in 1878 at the St. Stephen's Episcopal Church Normal and Industrial School. For 71 years it prepared black men for the ministry in the church. Giles B. Cooke (1838-1937) headed the vocational school and helped devel-

The Resurrection of Henry Box Brown. *Marker W-235. (New York Public Library Digital Collections)*

op the divinity school. In 1884 the school was named after the Rt. Rev. John Payne, the first bishop of Liberia. Prominent students included James Solomon Russell (1857-1935), who founded Saint Paul's College in Lawrenceville, and George Freeman Bragg Jr. (1853-1940), who became a priest and civil rights advocate. In 1949 the school merged with the Virginia Theological Seminary in Alexandria.

QA-38 CHARLES STEWART (CA. 1808–AFTER 1884)

On Pocahontas Street at Sapony Street. Charles Stewart, horseman, was born into slavery near Petersburg and spent part of his childhood on Pocahontas Island. At about the age of 12 he was sold to William R. Johnson, one of the foremost figures in horse racing, then America's most popular sport. Stewart succeeded as a jockey, trainer, stable manager, and stallion man, affording him money and fame. Artist Edward Troye painted his portrait with the stallion Medley in 1832. Johnson sent Stewart to run a stable in Kentucky in 1837 and later sold him to Alexander Porter, U.S. senator from Louisiana. Stewart then supervised Porter's highly regarded stables. *Harper's New Monthly Magazine* published Stewart's dictated memoir in 1884.

QA-26 CORLING'S CORNER

On N. Sycamore Street (Rte. 36) at W. Bank Street. By the 1820s, Petersburg was developing into a major industrial city. The backbone of the city's workforce was enslaved labor. At this highly visible downtown intersection known as Corling's Corner, local manufacturers, railroad companies, building contractors, and private individuals inspected and rented enslaved people to work for one-year terms in their businesses and homes.

Petersburg's tobacco factories were probably the largest users of rented labor. At the end of every year, enslaved men and women were hired under a legal contract that set forth the renter's obligations to the owner. The rental of bondspeople was quite common in the South before the Civil War.

QA-32 JOSEPH JENKINS ROBERTS (1809–1876)

Near corner of Wythe and Sycamore Streets. Joseph Jenkins Roberts, first president of Liberia, was born free in Norfolk. After moving to Petersburg, he worked in a barbershop at Wythe and Sycamore Streets and gained an education by reading extensively. In 1829 Roberts and his family sailed for Liberia, a settlement of the American Colonization Society. There he became a prosperous merchant. Elected president when Liberia won independence, he served from 1848 to 1856 and again from 1872 to 1876. He made several diplomatic visits to the U.S. Roberts helped found Liberia College (now the University of Liberia), and was its president for 20 years.

QA-39 LT. COL. HOWARD BAUGH, TUSKEGEE AIRMAN

At corner of N. Sycamore and Old Streets. Howard Baugh (1920-2008) was born and raised in Petersburg. He graduated from what is now Virginia State University in 1941, joined the U.S. Army Air Corps, and completed pilot training at Tuskegee Army Air Field in 1942. Deployed to Sicily with the 99th Fighter Squadron, Baugh flew 135 combat missions during World War II and was credited with 1.5 aerial victories. He later served as Director of Flying Training at Tuskegee. He was awarded the Distinguished Flying Cross, the Air Medal with 3 Oak Leaf Clusters, the French

Legion of Honor, and the Congressional Gold Medal. A 2006 Virginia Aviation Hall of Fame inductee, he was buried in Arlington National Cemetery with full military honors.

QA-27   PEABODY HIGH SCHOOL (1870–1970)

On Liberty Street at Harrison Street. Peabody High School, originally the Colored High School, was established in 1870 in the old First Baptist Church located on Harrison Street. The second school was built on Fillmore Street. The current site of the school is on Wesley Street. Peabody is one of the earliest publicly funded high schools for African Americans in Virginia. The city of Petersburg had begun to develop a public school system as early as 1868 and provided the funding needed to build city schools and pay teacher salaries. Alfred Pryor became the school's first African American principal in 1882.

QA-34   PEOPLE'S MEMORIAL CEMETERY

On S. Crater Road (Rte. 301) at St. Andrews Street.   Twenty-eight members of Petersburg's large community of free African Americans purchased a one-acre tract to serve as a burial ground in 1840. Subsequent acquisitions of adjacent land created a cemetery complex later known as People's Memorial. Buried here are slaves, an antislavery writer whose grave is listed on the National Underground Railroad Network to Freedom, a 19th-century member of the Virginia House of Delegates, veterans of the Civil War through World War II, and hundreds of other black residents. Numerous grave markers bearing the insignia of mutual aid societies and fraternal orders reflect the importance of these organizations to the community.

QA-35   POCAHONTAS ISLAND

On Sapony Street at Joseph Jenkins Roberts Street. The town of Pocahontas, established in 1752, became part of Petersburg in 1784. By 1860, more members of the city's large free African American community lived here than in any other neighborhood. Their work in tobacco factories and on wharves fueled the bustling Appomattox River trade.

Tuskegee Airmen circa May 1942 to August 1943. Location unknown, likely Southern Italy or North Africa. Markers JJ-34, JT-21, K-163, and QA-39. (US Air Force)

Residents likely used their access to the river to help enslaved blacks escape via the Underground Railroad. After the Civil War, Pocahontas attracted many emancipated African Americans. A tornado left widespread damage in 1993. The Jarratt House, ca. 1819, at 808-810 Logan Street, is the oldest standing structure. Archaeological evidence indicates Native American occupation of this area as early as 6500 BC.

QA-37   PRINCE HALL MASONS IN VIRGINIA

On Harrison Street between Liberty Street and South Avenue. In March 1775, a Masonic lodge attached to the British army initiated Prince Hall and 14 other free black men as Freemasons in Massachusetts. Meeting provisionally as African Lodge No. 1, the black Freemasons gained full privileges in 1787 when they organized African Lodge No. 459 under a charter from the Grand Lodge of England. The first affiliated lodge in Virginia was established in Alexandria in Feb. 1845. After the Civil War, two rival Grand Lodges operated in Virginia. On 15 Dec. 1875, these two Grand Lodges met at First Baptist Church–Harrison Street in Petersburg and united to form the present-day Most Worshipful Prince Hall Grand Lodge of Virginia, Free and Accepted Masons, Inc.

QA-28   UNDINE SMITH MOORE (1904–1989)

At 301 Halifax Street. Undine Smith Moore, educator and composer, was born in Jarratt and raised in Petersburg. Best known for her choral compositions, she was also a pianist and arranger. Her work often drew on African American sources such as spirituals. Moore's oratorio *Scenes from the Life of a Martyr*, a tribute to Dr Martin Luther King Jr., was nominated for a Pulitzer Prize. She attended Fisk University and earned a Master of Arts degree from Columbia University. She taught music at what is now Virginia State University from 1927 to 1972 and co-founded its Black Man in American Music program. Moore received the National Association of Negro Musicians' Distinguished Achievement Award in 1975.

QA-29   VIRGINIA VOTERS LEAGUE

On South Avenue between Harrison and Halifax Streets. The Virginia Voters League, founded in 1941 and headquartered in this neighborhood of Petersburg, was a federation of local organizations that advocated for African American voters. Professor Luther P. Jackson (of what is now Virginia State University), together with attorneys Robert H. Cooley Jr. and Raymond J. Valentine and educator James P. Spencer, organized the League, which allied itself with the NAACP and other civil rights organizations. The group educated its constituents about the rights of citizenship, promoted poll-tax payment and voter registration, and assuaged new voters' anxieties, leading to an increase in voter participation among African Americans.

POWHATAN COUNTY

O-71   POCAHONTAS HIGH SCHOOL

On Anderson Highway (Rte. 60) approximately 2500 feet west of Maidens Road (Rte. 522). Powhatan County established Powhatan Training School one mile southeast in 1931 to offer upper-level courses to African American students. In 1937 on this site the county built a brick high school for African Americans at a cost of about $40,000. The Federal Emergency Administration of Public Works, a New Deal agency, granted $18,000 for the project. Additional support came from the Virginia

Board of Education's Literary Fund and the Southern Education Foundation, which aided African American schools across the South. The building was named Pocahontas High School in 1941 and Pocahontas Middle School in 1969, when county schools were desegregated.

CITY OF RICHMOND

SA-69   ADAMS–VAN LEW HOUSE

At 2301 E. Grace Street.   Richmond mayor Dr. John Adams built a mansion here in 1802. It became the residence of Elizabeth Van Lew (1818–1900) whose father obtained it in 1836. During the Civil War, Elizabeth Van Lew led a Union espionage operation. African Americans, such as Van Lew's associate Mary Jane Richards (whose story closely parallels that of legendary spy Mary Elizabeth Bowser), served in Richmond's Unionist underground. Van Lew served as postmaster of Richmond from 1869 to 1877. Maggie Lena Walker, nationally known African American businesswoman, banker, and leader of the Independent Order of St. Luke, was born here by 1867. The house was razed in 1911 and in 1912 the Bellevue School was erected in its place.

SA-58   ALFRED D. "A. D." PRICE (CA. 1860–1921)

On E. Leigh Street (Rte. 33) at N. 2nd Street.   Alfred D. "A. D." Price, entrepreneur, spent his youth in Hanover County. After settling in Richmond in the 1870s, he opened a blacksmith shop ca. 1881 that expanded into a livery stable and undertaking business. He moved the enterprise to this site in 1898. In Aug. 1894, Price became one of the first funeral directors in Virginia to receive a state embalming license. That year he married Georgia A. Gibbons, a former contralto for the Fisk Jubilee Singers. Price invested in real estate and was a board member

for banks and other institutions. He was president of the Southern Aid Society of Virginia, a prominent minority-owned insurance company, from 1905 until his death on 9 Apr. 1921.

SA-48   BARTON HEIGHTS CEMETERIES

On St. James Street at intersection with School Street.   The Burying Ground Society of the Free People of Color of Richmond established its cemetery (later renamed Cedarwood) here in 1815. African Americans eventually founded five more cemeteries here: Union Burial Ground (later called Union Mechanics), Sons and Daughters of Ham, Ebenezer, Methodist, and Sycamore. The burial societies, fraternal orders, and religious organizations that sustained these cemeteries formed the cultural and economic bedrock of Richmond's nineteenth-century African American community. Here they gathered, especially on Whitmonday, to mourn the loss of revered figures and honor the memory of friends and family members, many of whom experienced the transition from slavery to freedom.

SA-77   CHARLES SIDNEY GILPIN

On W. Charity Street at intersection with St. Peter Street.   Charles Sidney Gilpin grew up here in Jackson Ward. He apprenticed in the *Richmond Planet* print shop before beginning his theater career and becoming one of the most highly regarded actors of the 1920s. Gilpin is best known for his title role in Eugene O'Neill's Broadway play *Emperor Jones*, for which he won the Drama League Award and the Spingarn Medal, and was named *Crisis* magazine Man of the Year (1921). The Drama League declared Gilpin one of ten people who had done the most for American theater. Gilpin was also honored at the White House during President Warren G. Harding's administration.

SA-97   DANIEL WEBSTER DAVIS
(1862–1913)

Dedication pending. Proposed location at 4401 Hobbs Lane.   D. Webster Davis, author, clergyman, and educator, was born into slavery in Caroline or Hanover County. He attended public school in Richmond after the Civil War and, beginning in 1879, taught in the city school system for 33 years. In 1887 Davis helped found the Virginia Teachers' Reading Circle, the state's first organization for African American educators. His book *Idle Moments, Containing Emancipation and Other Poems* (1895) reflected the challenges of his generation. He also wrote a book about African American history, was pastor of Second Baptist Church of Manchester, and traveled widely as a lecturer. Webster Davis Elementary School was formerly located near here at 4410 Northampton St.

SA-87   DOROTHY HEIGHT   (1912–2010)

At 1400 Hull Street.   Dorothy I. Height, civil rights leader, was born in Richmond and lived in this neighborhood until 1916. For more than 50 years she worked for racial justice and gender equality. Serving on the national staff of the Young Women's Christian Association (YWCA) from 1944 to 1977, Height fostered interracial dialogue and moved the YWCA toward full integration. As president of the National Council of Negro Women for 40 years, she promoted economic development and voting rights and advised United States presidents. She worked closely with Dr. Martin Luther King, Jr. and was a chief organizer of the March on Washington in 1963. Height was awarded the Presidential Medal of Freedom in 1994.

SA-96   EBENEZER BAPTIST CHURCH

At 216 W. Leigh Street.   Free blacks and slaves living west of Second St. and north of Broad St. founded the Third African Baptist Church in 1857. In 1858, it was dedicated on this site as Ebenezer Baptist Church, with a white minister, the Rev. William T. Lindsay, as pastor, as required by law. On 21 May 1865, the Rev. Peter Randolph became the congregation's first black pastor. The church made education one of its chief goals. It opened the first public school for black children in Richmond in 1866, organized Hartshorn Memorial College for black women in 1883, and helped found the Richmond Colored Young Men's Christian Association in 1887.

SA-54   ENGINE COMPANY NO. 9 FIRE STATION

On N. 5th Street at intersection with E. Duval Street.   On 1 July 1950, the first professional Afro-American firefighters in Virginia were hired and in September were stationed on the northeast corner of this intersection. These courageous pioneers created a loyalty and dedication to each other and their profession notwithstanding discriminatory practices. Harvey S. Hicks, among those first hired, became the city's first black fire captain in September 1961. On 14 June 1963, Hicks and firefighter Douglas P. Evans sacrificed their lives in a rescue attempt. The city integrated the fire department on 6 July 1963 and demolished the fire station in 1968.

SA-91   EVERGREEN CEMETERY

On E. Richmond Road approximately 900 feet east of Jennie Sher Road.   In 1891, Evergreen Cemetery was established as a preeminent resting place for many of Virginia's most influential African-American residents. These include Maggie L. Walker, president and founder of the St. Luke Penny Savings Bank, and John Mitchell, Jr., champion of African-American rights and editor of the *Richmond*

Planet newspaper. J. Henry Brown, a stonemason by trade, designed many of the tombstones erected here. By the early 1970s, the cemetery had fallen into disrepair. In 1975, volunteers from the Maggie L. Walker Historical Foundation led an effort to restore Evergreen to its original glory.

SA-66   EXECUTION OF GABRIEL

On E. Broad Street (Rte. 250) on the Shockoe Bottom viaduct.   Near here is the early site of the Richmond gallows and "Burial Ground for Negroes." On 10 Oct. 1800, Gabriel, an enslaved blacksmith from Brookfield plantation in Henrico County, was executed there for attempting to lead a mass uprising against slavery on 30 Aug. 1800. A fierce rainstorm delayed the insurrection, which then was betrayed by two slaves. Gabriel escaped and eluded capture until 23 Sept., when he was arrested in Norfolk. He was returned to Richmond on 27 Sept. and incarcerated in the Virginia State Penitentiary. On 6 Oct. he stood trial and was condemned. At least 25 of his supporters were also put to death there or in other jurisdictions.

SA-106   FIRST AFRICAN BAPTIST CHURCH

On E. Broad Street (Rte. 250) at College Street.   Tracing its roots to 1780 as the First Baptist Church, the First African Baptist Church was bought and organized by freedmen and slaves in 1841. The present building was erected on the same site in 1876. The establishment of First African Baptist Church led to the organization of other local black churches. In 1865, the site hosted the first Republican State Convention held in Virginia and Jefferson Davis's last speech as president of the Confederacy, and later a lecture by Booker T. Washington. The Rev. John Jasper, Henry "Box" Brown, and Maggie L. Walker were baptized at First African Baptist Church.

SA-107   FIRST SOUTHERN AFRICAN AMERICAN GIRL SCOUTS

On the campus of Virginia Union University in front of Hartshorn Hall.   In 1932, the first African American Girl Scout troop in the South began meeting nearby on the Virginia Union University campus. Sponsors of the troop included Lena Watson, Janie Jones, and Mary Virginia Binga. Girl Scouts enjoyed activities such as camp-

The First African American Girl Scout Troop in the South. Marker SA-107. (VCU Libraries)

ing, earning badges, and learning first aid. The Richmond Girl Scouts served as a model for other southern localities as the Girl Scout organization moved toward integration. Initially, Girl Scout activities in Virginia were segregated but by 1947 African American and white high school girls were working together on the Richmond Council newsletter.

SA-6   FREEDMEN'S BUREAU, FREEDMAN'S BANK

On N. 10th Street at intersection with Capitol Street.   Slavery denied African Americans the education and skills required to exercise the freedom won by the Civil War. To redress that, Congress created the Freedmen's Bureau and Freedman's Bank in March 1865. In Richmond, the Bureau and its branch Bank first operated out of two frame buildings here at 10th and Broad Streets, relocating several times before closing in 1872 and 1874, respectively. The agencies united families, legalized marriages, and provided education, food, clothing, job placement, legal and other services to former slaves. The Bureau's and Bank's written records are among the earliest and most complete histories of African American heritage.

SA-78   FRIENDS ASYLUM FOR COLORED ORPHANS

On W. Charity Street at intersection with St. Paul Street. Here stood the Friends Asylum for Colored Orphans. Lucy Goode Brooks and the Ladies Sewing Circle for Charitable Work, all formerly enslaved, founded it in 1871. The orphanage, supported by the Cedar Creek Meeting Society of Friends, provided a haven for orphaned African American children in post–Civil War Richmond. It was the only adoption agency in Virginia placing African American youth. Brooks's organization, now called

FRIENDS Association for Children, continues as a childcare and family support center. In 1970, it became a multi facility agency responding to the changing needs of the community. The original orphanage was demolished in 1969.

SA-76   GILES BEECHER JACKSON (CA. 1852–1924)

On N. 2nd Street at intersection with E. Clay Street.   The first African American to practice law before the Supreme Court of Virginia, Jackson lived and worked in Jackson Ward. Although local tradition holds that Jackson Ward was named for him, in fact, the ward's name first appeared during his childhood. In 1903 Jackson secured a charter from the Commonwealth of Virginia for the Negro Development and Exposition Company to facilitate the Negro Exhibit at the Jamestown Ter-Centennial Exposition in 1907. He helped organize the Southern Negro Business League as well as the Richmond Negro Exposition of 1915. Jackson also co-authored *The Industrial History of the Negro Race in Virginia*.

SA-74   JACKSON WARD

On N. 2nd Street between E. Clay and E. Leigh Streets.   Before the Civil War this neighborhood was home to free blacks and enslaved individuals, along with European immigrants and Jewish residents. The area served as a city electoral district (1871-1903) and is still called Jackson Ward. By the early 20th century it had become one of the premier centers of African American business, social, and residential life in the United States. Black-owned businesses such as the St. Luke Penny Savings Bank, the Southern Aid Insurance Company, the *Richmond Planet* newspaper, and Miller's Hotel (later Eggleston Hotel) thrived during legalized racial segregation. In the 1950s

The Negro Development and Exposition Co. of the U. S. A. Marker SA-76. (New York Public Library Digital Collections)

the new interstate highway bisected Jackson Ward. In 1978 the area became a National Historic Landmark.

SA-120   JAMES RIVER BATEAUMEN

Dedication pending. Proposed location at 301 Virginia Street.   The James River bateau, first used in the 1770s, was the primary means of transporting goods up and down the river between Richmond and points west until 1840, when the James River and Kanawha Canal was completed to Lynchburg. Crews of three men, often free or enslaved African Americans, performed the difficult and sometimes dangerous work of poling and steering the long, narrow boats. Largely unsupervised, bateaumen were entrusted with great responsibilities. They carried tobacco, grains, iron ore, coal, and other commodi-

ties to Richmond, helping to make the city a hub for industry and commerce. Traffic typically terminated at the Great Basin, built in 1800 1/5 mile northwest of here.

SA-61   JOHN MILLER HOUSE

On Holly Street between S. Pine and S. Belvedere Streets.   John Miller, a free black cooper and minister, built this house about 1858. It is significant as a rare surviving antebellum house in Richmond constructed by and for a free African American family. More than two thousand free blacks lived in Richmond at the time of the Civil War; at least two hundred of them were homeowners. Miller was an influential member of the small free black community that existed in present-day Oregon Hill. Originally erected at 614 S. Laurel Street, the dwelling moved to its present location in 1917, two blocks to the west of here at 617 S. Cherry Street, by Richmond businessman Moses Nunnally.

SA-73   JOHN MITCHELL, JR., "FIGHTING EDITOR"

On N. 3rd Street between E. Marshall and E. Clay Streets.   Born enslaved near Richmond in 1863, John Mitchell, Jr. came of age in the tumultuous post–Civil War era. In 1883, he launched a daring journalism career, becoming editor and publisher of the black-owned *Richmond Planet* once located near here. Known as the "Fighting Editor," Mitchell crusaded against lynching, served on the Richmond City Council (1888–1896) and founded the Mechanics Savings Bank in 1902. In 1904, he led a boycott of Richmond's segregated streetcars. In 1921, he ran for governor to protest black disfranchisement. Mitchell served as *Planet* editor until his death in 1929. He is buried in Evergreen Cemetery.

John Mitchell, Jr., Marker SA-73. (Library of Virginia)

SA-102   LEIGH STREET ARMORY

At 122 W. Leigh Street (Rte. 33).   In 1895, the city of Richmond constructed the Leigh Street or First Battalion Virginia Volunteers Armory, the nation's only 19th-century armory built for an African American militia. Several decades of noteworthy performance by Virginia's black militia combined with tireless lobbying by *Richmond Planet* editor John Mitchell, Jr., contributed to the city's decision to fund the armory. After 1899, when Virginia's governor disbanded black militia units, the armory served until 1981 primarily as a school for black children: Monroe Elementary School, Colored Special School, Graves Junior High School annex, and Armstrong High School annex. During World War II, it served as a reception center for black soldiers.

E-232   LOVING V. VIRGINIA

At 1111 E. Broad Street (Rte. 250).   Richard Loving and Mildred Jeter, defined under Virginia's 1924 Racial Integrity Act as an interracial couple, married in June 1958 in Washington, D.C., and returned home to Caroline County. Arrested in July for violating Virginia's laws against interracial marriage, the Lovings were convicted and sentenced to one year in jail, suspended on the condition that they leave Virginia. In 1963 they obtained help from the American Civil Liberties Union, which unsuccessfully sought to reverse their convictions in the state courts of Virginia and then appealed to the U.S. Supreme Court, which, in the case *Loving v. Virginia* (1967), overturned all state laws restricting marriage on the basis of race.

SA-105   MILLER'S AND EGGLESTON HOTELS

At 541 N. 2nd Street.   Opened in 1904 and demolished in 2009, the hotel that stood here hosted regional and national black luminaries, celebrities, tourists, and leaders including Booker T. Washington. Built by William "Buck" Miller, Miller's Hotel was one of a handful in Richmond to offer black customers fine accommodations, a rarity in the segregated South. Its success reflected the entrepreneurial and professional efforts of the residents of Jackson Ward, widely considered "The Birthplace of Black Capitalism." Under subsequent owner Neverett Eggleston, the renamed Eggleston Hotel was a hotspot beginning in 1943, hosting such entertainers as Louis Armstrong, Count Basie, and Redd Foxx.

SA-85   NAVY HILL

At the intersection of Jackson and N. 4th Streets.   The Navy Hill neighborhood, named as a tribute to nearby naval victories during the War of 1812, was settled by German immigrants beginning in 1810. It became a vibrant African American community by the turn of the century. Navy Hill's distinctive character was embodied in the buildings here between North Third and Thirteenth Streets. Navy Hill School was the only Richmond public school to employ black teachers. Area landmarks included the Bill "Bojangles" Robinson home, Good Samaritan Society, Phyllis Wheatley YMCA, and numerous churches. The construction of Interstate 95 destroyed Navy Hill in the 1960s.

SA-8   OLIVER WHITE HILL SR. (1907–2007)

Dedication pending.   Oliver White Hill Sr., civil rights attorney, helped dismantle legally mandated racial segregation in the South. He graduated from the Howard University School of Law in 1933 and returned to Richmond, his native city, in 1939. Working for the Virginia NAACP, he challenged inequities in education, public facilities, voting rights, and the criminal justice system. One of his cases was consolidated into the U.S. Supreme Court's *Brown v. Board of Education* decision (1954). In 1948, Hill became the first African American elected to the Richmond City Council in the 20th century. The Finance Building in Capitol Square was renamed for him in 2005.

SA-83   RICHMOND 34

On E. Broad Street (Rte. 250) between N. 6th and N. 7th Streets. On 22 Feb. 1960, 34 Virginia Union University students, 11 women and 23 men, refused to leave the segregated dining facilities here at Thalhimers department store and were arrested. Charged with trespassing, they were later convicted and fined. This sit-in was part of a wave of protests across the South inspired by recent sit-ins in

Greensboro, North Carolina. The arrests of the Richmond 34 sparked the Campaign for Human Dignity, which organized boycotts and picketed Richmond businesses. Thalhimers and other retailers subsequently desegregated. In June 1963 the U.S. Supreme Court overturned the convictions of the Richmond 34 in *Randolph v. Virginia.*

SA-65   RICHMOND'S FIRST AFRICAN AMERICAN POLICE OFFICERS

At the intersection of W. Leigh Street (Rte. 33) and Brook Road. On 1 May 1946, Richmond's first professional African American police officers were hired and assigned to the First Precinct at Smith and Marshall Streets. They were Howard T. Braxton, Doctor P. Day, Frank S. Randolph, and John W. Vann. On 16 December 1949, Ruth B. Blair became the first professional African American female police officer hired and assigned to the Juvenile Division. On 18 July 1964, Sergeant Randolph was promoted to Detective Lieutenant. While challenged by segregated conditions and discriminatory practices, their perseverance created an inspiring legacy.

SA-79   SAINT JOSEPH CATHOLIC CHURCH

On N. 1st Street between E. Jackson and E. Duval Streets. In 1884, Bishop John Keane bought this property and established Saint Joseph, making it the first-known Catholic congregation organized for African Americans in Virginia. The original congregation began in the basement of the all-white Saint Peter's Church in 1879, and grew to 50 members. During the years 1904–1968, this site also contained the Franciscan convent, still standing, Saint Mary's; a two-room school for grades K–12, later named Van de Vyver; a parish house; a trade school; and a two-year business college, Van de Vyver Institute. In 1969, the church

One of the 34 Virginia Union University students arrested for "trespassing" at Thalhimers department store in Richmond. Marker SA-83. (Richmond Times Dispatch)

and the school were formally closed by Bishop John J. Russell.

SA-98 SAMUEL L. GRAVELY JR. (1922–2004)

Dedication pending. Proposed location in the 800 block of Old Nicholson Street. Samuel L. Gravely Jr., a pioneering naval officer, spent his early years near here at 819 Nicholson Street in Fulton. He enlisted in the U.S. Navy Reserve in 1942 and in Dec. 1944 became the first African American commissioned as a Navy Reserve officer. During his 38-year career he became the first African American naval officer to command a warship, command a fleet, and attain the ranks of rear admiral and vice admiral. After serving in World War II, the Korean War, and the Vietnam War, Gravely retired from the Navy in 1980. He is buried at Arlington National Cemetery.

SA-43 SIXTH MOUNT ZION BAPTIST CHURCH

At 14 W. Duval Street.   The Rev. John Jasper, born a slave in Fluvanna County on 4 July 1812, organized the Sixth Mount Zion Baptist Church congregation in Richmond on 3 Sept. 1867 in a former Confederate stable on Brown's Island. A nationally celebrated preacher, Jasper was best known for his 1878 sermon "De Sun Do Move," which he later delivered by invitation more than 250 times. He died on 30 Mar. 1901 and is buried in Woodlawn Cemetery in Richmond. In 1869, the congregation moved to this site. The present church (built 1887-1890) was remodeled in 1925 in the Gothic Revival style by the noted black architect Charles T. Russell.

SA-1 SPOTTSWOOD W. ROBINSON III (1916–1998)

Dedication pending.   Spottswood W. Robinson III, a Richmond native, fought against Jim Crow laws that made African Americans second-class citizens. An attorney, he worked for the Virginia NAACP and the NAACP Legal Defense and Educational Fund and helped to argue a school desegregation case that culminated in the U.S. Supreme Court decision in *Brown v. Board of Education* (1954). Robinson was dean of the Howard University School of Law from 1960 to 1963. He became the first African American to serve as a judge on the U.S. District Court for the District of Columbia (1964-66), and was later the first to sit on the U.S. Court of Appeals for the District of Columbia as a judge (1966-81) and as chief judge (1981-86).

Judge Spottswood W. Robinson, III. Marker SA-1. (Courtesy of Oswald and Nina Robinson Govan)

SA-121 THE WESTWOOD COMMUNITY

Dedication pending. Proposed location: intersection of Dunbar Street, Willow Lawn Drive, and Patterson Avenue.   Formerly enslaved African Americans established Westwood Village here after the Civil War. Residents built houses, a church, a school, and businesses, forming a vibrant, self-sustaining community with many social and cultural organizations. The City of Richmond annexed Westwood from Henrico County in 1942. In the mid-1940s, residents resisted several attempts by the city to demolish the community and replace it with a park. Residents also combated segregation in Richmond's public schools. A student from Westwood became the first African American to attend Westhampton Junior High (in 1961) and Thomas Jefferson High (in 1962) after a federal court decision in *Warden v. Richmond School Board.*

SA-41 UNION ARMY ENTERS RICHMOND

At the intersection of E. Main Street (Rte. 5) and Old Main Street.   Here Maj. Gen. Godfrey Weitzel, commander of the Army of the James, entered and took possession of Richmond at 8:15 A.M. on 3 April 1865 after receiving the surrender of the confederate capital from Mayor Joseph Mayo a few miles east. The first units of Weitzel's command to enter the city were six regiments from Brig. Gen. Edward H. Ripley's 1st Brigade of the XXIVth Army Corps, and U.S. Colored Troops from infantry and cavalry regiments of the XXVth Army Corps. During the next twenty-four hours, the Union troops extinguished the fire that destroyed almost 40 blocks extending along the river and north to Capitol Square, restored order, and occupied Confederate office buildings.

James L. Farmer. Marker E-113. (LBJ Library photo by Yoichi Okamoto)

SPOTSYLVANIA COUNTY

E-113   JAMES FARMER, CIVIL RIGHTS
LEADER

*At the intersection of Jefferson Davis
Highway (Rte. 1) and Guinea Station Road
(Rte. 607).*   James Leonard Farmer was
born in Texas on 12 Jan. 1920. In 1942, he
and other Civil Rights leaders founded the
Congress of Racial Equality (CORE) in Chicago. CORE used Gandhi-inspired tactics
of nonviolent civil disobedience to protest
discriminatory practices against blacks.
Under Farmer's leadership, in the spring of
1961, CORE organized "Freedom Riders" to
desegregate interstate transportation in the
Deep South. He was an assistant secretary
in the U.S. Department of Health, Education and Welfare (1969-1970). Farmer
taught at Mary Washington College (1985-
1999) and received the Presidential Medal
of Freedom in 1998. Farmer died on 9 July
1999. His house stands east of here.

EM-4   JOHN J. WRIGHT SCHOOL

*Dedication pending. Proposed location at
7565 Courthouse Road (Rte. 208).*
Representatives from local African American churches organized the Spotsylvania
Sunday School Union in 1905 to secure a
secondary school for black children. The
Union, led by educator John J. Wright, purchased 158.5 acres here in 1910 and later
deeded 20 acres to the county. The Snell
Training School, built by Alfred Fairchild,
opened here in 1913 and was for decades
the county's only public high school for
black students. Renamed for John J. Wright
in 1940, it burned in 1941 and was rebuilt
in 1952. The building became a middle
school in 1968 after desegregation was
completed. In 2008, after a major renova-
tion, the building was designated the John
J. Wright Educational and Cultural Center.

EM-3 23RD USCT AT THE ALRICH FARM

At the intersection of Catharpin Road (Rte. 612) with Sawhill Boulevard. The first combat in the Civil War between United States Colored Troops and Confederates north of the James River occurred near here. On 15 May 1864, Confederate Brig. Gen. Thomas Rosser pushed forward a cavalry detachment along Catharpin Road to determine the position of the Union army. His men encountered—and pushed back—the 2nd Ohio Cavalry. To support the cavalry, the nearby 23rd United States Colored Infantry hurried forward to the intersection of Catharpin Road and Orange Plank Road. After skirmishing with the Confederates, the 23rd charged and caused Rosser to withdraw.

Virginian Sgt. Nimrod Burke (1836–1914) of Company F, 23rd U.S. Colored Infantry. Marker EM-3. (Virginia Humanities)

A student of shipbuilding at Newport News photographed by Frances Benjamin Johnston c. 1895. (Library of Congress)

REGION FOUR

Eastern Virginia

Accomack County

Charles City County

City of Chesapeake

Essex County

City of Franklin

Gloucester County

City of Hampton

James City County

King William County

Mathews County

Middlesex County

New Kent County

City of Newport News

City of Norfolk

Northampton County

City of Portsmouth

Southampton County

City of Suffolk

Surry County

Sussex County

City of Virginia Beach

City of Williamsburg

York County

ACCOMACK COUNTY

Q-83 FORT ALBION

On Tangier Island on Main Ridge Road between Chambers and Thomas Roads. In April 1814, during the War of 1812, British forces commanded by Adm. Sir George Cockburn established Fort Albion on the southern tip of Tangier Island. The fort, which included barracks, a hospital, a church, parade grounds, and gardens, housed hundreds of African Americans who had gained their freedom by escaping to the British. Many of them enlisted as Colonial Marines and received military training here. From this base the British launched raids up and down the Chesapeake Bay, including those on Washington, D.C., and Baltimore. In March 1815 they left the island and destroyed the fort. The site is now under water.

EP-22   MARY NOTTINGHAM SMITH HIGH SCHOOL

In Accomac at the intersection of Front Street (Rte. 13 Alt.) with T. C. Walker Drive.   The first high school for blacks in Accomack County was dedicated on this site in 1932. It was named in honor of Mary Nottingham Smith (1892-1951), a black educator who dedicated her life to educating all young people. In 1956, the school was renamed for T. C. Walker, an attorney from Gloucester County. It was demolished in 1987. A second Mary N. Smith High School was built on another site in 1953.

CHARLES CITY COUNTY

V-34   FORT POCAHONTAS

On John Tyler Memorial Highway (Rte. 5) approximately 700 feet east of Sturgeon Point Road (Rte. 614).   South of here, on a bluff overlooking the James River, stands the half-mile-long Fort Pocahon-tas, built in the spring of 1864 by Union soldiers during the Civil War. The fort protected Union vessels on the river and guarded the landing at Wilson's Wharf. Commanded by Brig. Gen. Edward A. Wild and manned by the 1st and 10th Regiments of U.S. Colored Troops and two guns of Battery M, 3d N.Y. Light Artillery, the 1,500-man garrison beat back assaults by 2,500 cavalrymen under Confederate Maj. Gen. Fitzhugh Lee on 24 May 1864. It was the only Civil War battle in Virginia in which nearly all the Union troops were black.

V-54   ISAAC BRANDON LYNCHED, 6 APRIL 1892

On Courthouse Road (Rte. 644) at Court House Green Way.   A mob of about 75 masked men dragged Isaac Brandon from a cell in the old Charles City County jail and hanged him from a tree on this hillside on the night of 6 April 1892. Brandon, a 43-year-old black man, had been held in jail on a charge of assaulting a white woman. He was married and the father of eight children. No charges were filed in connection with Brandon's murder. More than 4,000 lynchings took place in the United States between 1877 and 1950. In Virginia, approximately 100 people, the vast majority of them black men, were killed in documented lynchings. Lynch mobs terrorized African Americans and helped to maintain white supremacy.

V-27   LOTT CARY BIRTHPLACE

On Courthouse Road (Rte. 155) approximately 100 feet north of Lott Cary Road.   A mile and a half northwest, Lott Cary was born in slavery about 1780. In 1804 his owner, John Bowry, a Methodist minister, hired him out to a Richmond tobacco firm. Cary joined the First Baptist Church in 1807. He purchased his freedom and became a Baptist minister in 1813, then founded the African Missionary Society in 1815. Cary sailed for Africa in 1821 as the continent's first African-American missionary. He established Providence Baptist Church in Monrovia, Liberia, and several schools. As a political and military leader, Cary helped Liberia survive as a colony of free American blacks. He died there in November 1828.

CITY OF CHESAPEAKE

WP-13 JUSTIN HOLLAND

At the intersection of Shell Road and George Washington Highway N. (Bus. Rte. 17).   Justin Holland was a 19th-century pioneer African American of the classical guitar, community leader, and abolitionist. Born in Norfolk County about 1819, he left for Massachusetts in 1833. There he took music lessons and learned to play the guitar. He moved to Cleveland, Ohio, in the 1840s, became a music teacher, and arranged several hundred pieces of music for the guitar. He also played an active role in the movement to secure equal rights for African Americans and attended the first National Negro Convention in Philadelphia in 1830. He died at his son's home in New Orleans on 24 Mar. 1887.

ESSEX COUNTY

N-39 BRITISH RAID ON TAPPAHANNOCK

In Tappahannock on Queen Street (Rte. 360) between Newbill Drive and Water Lane.   On 2 Dec. 1814, British naval forces commanded by Capt. Robert Barrie shelled and seized the town of Tappahannock during the War of 1812. Aiding the British were three companies of Colonial Marines composed of formerly enslaved African Americans. By 4 Dec., when the raiders departed and Essex County militia reentered the town, the British had ransacked private houses, blown up a tan-nery, and burned two jails, the customs warehouse, and the courthouse. They also desecrated the burial vault of the prominent Ritchie family. This was one of the last British raids before the Treaty of Ghent was signed on 24 Dec. 1814.

N-26 MANN MEETING HOUSE

Tidewater Trail (Rte. 17 northbound) between Oakley and Center Cross.   Just to the east stood Mann Meeting House, the first Methodist Episcopal Church in this region. It was built before 1794 and abandoned about 1880. The site is now occupied by the Macedonia Colored Baptist Church.

N-37 WILLIAM MOORE--TIDEWATER MUSICIAN

In Tappahannock on Church Lane (Rte. 17) between Parker Place and Marsh Street.   William "Bill" Moore was born in Georgia in 1893. Nearby stood his home and barbershop. Paramount recorded Moore in Chicago in 1928 and released eight songs, some of the earliest by an African American folk performer from Virginia. They are still valued and performed by musicians. "Old Country Rock," a dance tune, refers to the Rappahannock River and the town of Tappahannock, while "Barbershop Rag" testifies to his fine ragtime guitar style and his profession. Moore also performed blues for his customers and dance audiences as well as popular songs such as "Ragtime Millionaire." He died in Fauquier County in 1951 and is buried in the Warrenton Cemetery.

CITY OF FRANKLIN

U-133   DELLA IRVING HAYDEN
(CA. 1855–1924)

At 580 Oak Street.   Della I. Hayden, educator, was born into slavery in North Carolina and moved to Virginia with her mother after the Civil War. She attended a Freedmen's Bureau school and graduated from the Hampton Normal and Agricultural Institute (later Hampton University) in 1877. She then served as a teacher and principal in Franklin and, for more than a decade, was "lady principal" of what is now Virginia State University. In 1904 Hayden founded the Franklin Normal and Industrial Institute to provide academic, agricultural, and industrial training to African American students. The school, renamed Hayden High School in her honor, moved into a new brick building here in 1953.

U-132   PAULINE CAUTHORNE MORTON
(1912–2004)

At 280 N. College Drive.   Pauline C. Morton, civic leader, graduated from what is now Virginia State University in 1933. She began working for the Virginia Department of Education in 1947, during the segregation era. Before retiring in 1974, she supervised home economics education across southeastern Virginia and implemented the federal school lunch program in her region. Morton was Mid-Atlantic Regional Director of Alpha Kappa Alpha Sorority, the first Greek-letter organization for African American women. She helped organize the Franklin NAACP chapter in 1943, chaired the Franklin City Public School Board and the board of Paul D. Camp Community College, and served on more than 20 other civic committees.

GLOUCESTER COUNTY

NW-20   BETHEL BAPTIST CHURCH

At 2978 Hickory Fort Road (Rte. 616). Bethel Baptist Church is one of the oldest African American congregations in Gloucester County. Founded nearby in 1867, it was originally known as the Old Sassafras Stage Church. Members of the congregation built a wooden structure here in 1889, which is the core of the present building. George W. Leigh and Thomas C. Walker, Sr., father of Thomas C. Walker, Jr., served as chairmen of the building committee. During the later years of the 19th century five other churches were organized from this congregation. Thomas C. Walker, Jr. (1862-1953), the first black lawyer in Gloucester County, is buried in the adjoining church cemetery.

NW-18   GLOUCESTER AGRICULTURAL AND INDUSTRIAL SCHOOL

On Cappahosic Road (Rte. 618) approximately 250 feet east of Foxhaven Drive. On this site stood the Gloucester Agricultural and Industrial School, commonly known as Capahosic Academy, a private high school built for African Americans before public high schools were available to them. Founded in 1888 by local alumni of Hampton Institute (now Hampton University), it was taken over and funded by the American Missionary Association after 1891. William Gibbons Price (1868?-1941) was the principal from 1899 until it closed in 1933. Despite the school's name, graduates included not only well-trained farmers, but also many students who attended college and entered professions such as teaching. It was a cultural center of the local black community.

NW-21   GLOUCESTER TRAINING SCHOOL

At 6099 T. C. Walker Road (Rte. 629). Built on this site in 1921 the Gloucester Training School became the first public high school for African Americans in Gloucester County. Thomas Calhoun Walker, Jr. and others constructed a wooden building with gifts from the Rosenwald Fund and other national and local donors. It offered African Americans an education beyond the elementary school level. A new brick structure replaced the original building by 1951 and was named for Walker in 1954. Following the integration of the county schools, the school in 1968 became Gloucester Intermediate School. The building became a middle school in 1975 and in 1986 it was named T. C. Walker Elementary School.

NW-12   ROBERT RUSSA MOTON

On George Washington Memorial Highway (Rte. 17) approximately 150 feet south of intersection with Hickory Fork Road (Rte. 614).   Robert Russa Moton was born in Amelia County, Virginia, on 26 August 1867, and was educated in a local freedman's school and at Hampton Institute (now Hampton University). He served as an administrator at the institute from 1890 to 1915, when he succeeded Booker T. Washington as president of Tuskegee Institute. There Moton led the school to full collegiate accreditation. An advisor to five U.S. presidents and a founder of the Urban League, he retired to Holly Knoll (10 miles northwest) in 1935. Moton died on 31 May 1940. Holly Knoll was designated a National Historic Landmark in 1981.

NW-7   THE IRENE MORGAN STORY BEGINS

Dedication pending. Proposed location: 2425 Hayes Road.   On this site stood the Hayes Store Post Office, where Irene Morgan boarded a Greyhound bus on 16 July 1944. Morgan, an African American woman, was returning home to Baltimore, MD, after visiting her mother. About 25 miles north of here, the bus driver ordered her to give up her seat so

that white passengers could sit. Refusing to comply, she was arrested and jailed in Saluda, VA. Her case reached the U.S. Supreme Court, which decided in *Morgan v. Virginia* (1946) that laws requiring the segregation of passengers in interstate transportation were unconstitutional. Morgan took her stand 11 years before Rosa Parks in Montgomery, AL.

NW-11   THOMAS CALHOUN WALKER (1862–1953)

In Gloucester on Main Street (Rte. 17) approximately 500 north of John Clayton Memorial Highway (Rte. 3).   Here lived Thomas Calhoun Walker, the first black to practice law in Gloucester County and a civil rights spokesman who vigorously advocated education and land ownership for blacks. Mr. Walker was elected for two terms to Gloucester's Board of Supervisors, serving from 1891 to 1895. President William McKinley appointed him the Commonwealth's first black collector of customs in 1893. He became the only black to hold statewide office in President Roosevelt's Works Project Administration when he was appointed Consultant and Advisor on Negro Affairs in 1934.

NW-13   UNITED NEGRO COLLEGE FUND

On George Washington Memorial Highway (Rte. 17) approximately 150 feet south of Hickory Fork Road (Rte. 614). Dr. Frederick D. Patterson founded the United Negro College Fund in 1944. He and the presidents of the member colleges of the Fund began meeting in 1946 at Holly Knoll, the retirement home of the late Robert Russa Moton. Patterson had established Holly Knoll Associates in 1945 to serve as a conference center for black educators. Their meetings contributed to the growth and reputation of the United Negro College Fund, which aids more than 40 historically black colleges,

President Lyndon Johnson meeting with Dr. Frederick Patterson, President of the United Negro College Fund. Marker NW-13. (LBJ Library photo by Cecil Stoughton)

and provides student scholarships and faculty grants. The fund is known for its motto, "A mind is a terrible thing to waste."

NW-17 Zion Poplars Baptist Church

At 7000 T. C. Walker Road (Rte. 629).
Zion Poplars Baptist Church houses one of the oldest independent African-American congregations in Gloucester County. It is named for seven united poplar trees under which the founding members first met for worship in 1866. The church was erected here in 1894 in the Gothic Revival architectural style, with both Victorian and classical detailing. During the 1930s the church was moved 110 feet because of road construction. The interior exhibits the creative craftsmanship of Frank Braxton, a former slave. The church was listed on the Virginia Landmarks Register and the National Register of Historic Places in 1999. *Note: NW-16, a duplicate of NW-17, is located on US 17 about a mile south of Belroi Road.*

CITY OF HAMPTON

W-95 Aberdeen Gardens

At 1424 Aberdeen Road.   Built "by Negroes, for Negroes," Aberdeen Gardens began in 1934 as the model resettlement community for Negro families. It was the only such community in the United States designed by a Negro architect (Hilyard R. Robinson) and built by Negro contractors and laborers. Aberdeen Gardens is composed of 158 brick houses on large garden lots, a school, and a community store, all within a greenbelt. The streets, excepting Aberdeen Road, are named for prominent Negroes. Aberdeen Gardens offered home ownership and an improved quality of life in a rural setting. In 1994 this nationally significant neighborhood was listed as a Virginia landmark and in the National Register of Historic Places, through the efforts of former and current residents.

W-107 BAY SHORE HOTEL

At 330 S. Resort Boulevard. Bay Shore Hotel opened here in 1898 as a cooperative venture by 60 African Americans to establish a coastal resort for blacks from across the South during the segregation era. Ravaged by an Aug. 1933 hurricane, it was rebuilt and operated until 1973. It had a dance pavilion, café, private beach, and amusement park, and hosted state and national conferences, sporting events, and concerts, along with honeymoons, family vacations, and day trips. Jazz greats Cab Calloway, Ella Fitzgerald, Louis Armstrong, and Duke Ellington performed here, and pioneering African American groups, the American Bridge Association and Tri-State Dental Association, now the National Dental Association, held their founding meetings here.

WY-98 DEAF AND BLIND SCHOOL

At the intersection of Old Aberdeen and Shell Roads. In 1906, the Virginia General Assembly authorized the Virginia School for Colored Deaf and Blind Children. Founded by deaf humanitarian William C. Ritter and Hampton Delegate Harry R. Houston, the school opened on 8 Sept. 1909 to serve students from throughout Virginia. More than 100 acres were eventually purchased or donated for buildings used for instruction, dormitories, an infirmary, a farm, and other facilities for academic and vocational training programs. Desegregated by 1964, after several name changes the school was renamed The Virginia School for the Deaf, Blind and Multi-disabled at Hampton in 2000.

W-173 DOROTHY JOHNSON VAUGHAN (1910–2008)

Dedication pending. Location pending. Dorothy Vaughan, mathematician, graduated from Wilberforce University in Ohio and was a member of Alpha Kappa Alpha Sorority. During World War II she left her job as a teacher to work for the National Advisory Committee for Aeronautics (NACA), later NASA, at the Langley Memorial Aeronautical Laboratory near Hampton. She was assigned to the West Area Computing Unit, a group of African American women responsible for processing aeronautical research data. In 1949, Vaughan became NACA's first African American supervisor. She excelled at the FORTRAN computer

Aberdeen Gardens Historic District. Marker W-95. (DHR 114-0146)

Dorothy Johnson Vaughan. Marker W-173. (NASA)

programming language and contributed to the Scout launch vehicle project, a crucial component of the space program, before retiring in 1971.

W-98 EMANCIPATION OAK

On Settlers Landing Road (Rte. 60) at entrance ramp to I-64 East. To the west, on the grounds of Hampton University, stands the Emancipation Oak. Under its sheltering limbs, protected and encouraged by the occupying Union army and prominent local church leaders, Mary Smith Kelsey Peake (1823-22 Feb. 1862) taught her fellow African Americans to read and write as the Civil War began. She founded the first black school in Hampton at Brown Cottage in September 1861; it was a forerunner of Hampton University. In 1863, following the issuance of the Emancipation Proclamation by President Abraham Lincoln, Hampton residents gathered beneath the oak to hear the text read aloud.

W-96 FIRST AFRICANS IN VIRGINIA

On Fenwick Road approximately 800 feet east of Ingalls Road. The first documented Africans in Virginia arrived here in Aug. 1619 on the *White Lion*, an English privateer based in the Netherlands. Colonial officials traded food for these "20 and odd" Africans, who had been captured from a Portuguese slave ship. Among present-day Hampton's earliest African residents were Antony and Isabella. Their son, William, was the first child of African ancestry known to have been born in Virginia (ca. 1624). Many of the earliest Africans were held as slaves, but some individuals became free. A legal framework for hereditary, lifelong slavery in Virginia evolved during the 1600s. The United States abolished slavery in 1865.

W-94 FREEDOM'S FORTRESS

On Ruckman Road at Fort Monroe National Monument. Fort Monroe was the site of Major General Benjamin F. Butler's decision in 1861 to accept escaping slaves as "contrabands of war." Thousands of former slaves who cast off their bondage and sought sanctuary here called this "The Freedom Fort." The First and Second Regiments of U.S. Colored Cavalry and Battery B, Second U.S. Colored Light Artillery, were raised here during the Civil War. In 1865 the Bureau for the Relief of Freedmen and Refugees ("Freedmen's Bureau") established its state headquarters here.

S-28 JOHN BAPTIST PIERCE (1875–1942)

On Settlers Landing Road (Rte. 60) between William R. Harvey Way and on-ramp to I-64 East. A Cooperative Extension Service pioneer, innovator, and educator, John Baptist Pierce was appointed in 1906 by Seaman Knapp and H. B. Frissell of Hampton Institute as the first Negro farm demonstration agent for Virginia. Pierce served for 35 years as district agent for Virginia and North Carolina and as the United States Department of Agriculture field agent for the upper southern states. Pierce's "Live-at-Home and Community Improvement Program" was a unique innovation which helped many rural Virginians raise their standards of living.

WY-95 LITTLE ENGLAND CHAPEL

At intersection of Kecoughtan Road (Rte. 60) and Ivy Home Road.   Little England Chapel, originally known as the Ocean Cottage Sunday School, was built about 1879 on property provided by Daniel F. Cock. Hampton Institute students regularly offered Sunday school lessons here to the African American Newtown community from the early 1880s into the 20th century. By 1890 the chapel had become known for its sewing club. The Newtown Improvement and Civic Club also held meetings at the chapel and programs of worship, singing, and concerts took place here. The club acquired the property in 1954. The church was listed on the Virginia Landmarks Register in 1981 and the National Register of Historic Places in 1982.

W-97 MARY SMITH KELSEY PEAKE

At intersection of Wine Street and Poplar Avenue.   Born a free person in Norfolk in 1823, Mary Peake devoted her life to the education and betterment of African Americans. About 1850, she founded the Daughters of Zion to aid the poor and the sick. A seamstress by day, Peake violated state law to teach her fellow blacks at night. During the Civil War, protected and encouraged by the occupying Union army and prominent local leaders, she taught openly in the shade of the Emancipation Oak in Hampton and at Fort

Mary Jackson working at NASA Langley. Marker W-174. (NASA)

Monroe. She founded the first black school in Hampton at Brown Cottage in September 1861 with the sponsorship of the American Missionary Association. Her school was a forerunner of Hampton University. Peake died on 22 February 1862.

W-174 MARY WINSTON JACKSON (1920–2015)

Dedication pending. Location pending. Mary Jackson, aerospace engineer, was born in Hampton and graduated from Hampton Institute in 1942. The National Advisory Committee for Aeronautics (NACA), later NASA, hired her in 1951 to be a "human computer" in the segregated West Area Computing Unit at Langley Aeronautical Laboratory. In 1958 she became NASA's first African American female engineer. Her research focused on airflow around aircraft, and she contributed to Projects Mercury and Apollo. Jackson later worked to advance the careers of other female engineers and scientists. She was a member of Alpha Kappa Alpha Sorority, a Girl Scout leader, and a volunteer in many civic organizations.

W-106 VIRGINIA STATE FEDERATION OF COLORED WOMEN'S CLUBS

At 123 E. Pembroke Avenue.   This house was the last headquarters of the Virginia State Federation of Colored Women's Clubs, organized in 1907 by educator and social reformer Janie Porter Barrett and other women who attended the annual Hampton Negro Conference. The Federation fostered cooperation among the state's many African American women's clubs, which had emerged late in the 19th century to address the needs of women and children and to improve education, health care, home life, and economic opportunity. In 1915 the Federation opened the Industrial Home School for Colored Girls, a rehabilitation center in Hanover County for girls in legal trouble.

JAMES CITY COUNTY

WT-4 COMMUNITY OF GROVE

At intersection of Pocahontas Trail (Rte. 60) and Magruder Avenue. After the Civil War, in the area that later became known as the Community of Grove, the Freedmen's Bureau confiscated land for displaced newly freed slaves and free blacks. In 1867, the government restored the land to its previous owners. Some African American residents moved to and settled on lands that became known locally as the Reservation and the Banks. In 1918, their descendants returned to the area of Grove after the U.S. government forced their removal to make way for the Yorktown Naval Weapons Station and the Cheatham Annex. The expansion of these facilities during World War II led to the further growth of Grove.

WT-1 FIRST AFRICANS IN JAMESTOWN

On Jamestown Road (Rte. 31) at Capital Trail crosswalk to Greensprings Road. The first documented Africans in mainland English America arrived at Point Comfort (in present-day Hampton) late in Aug. 1619. Colonial officials traded food for these "20 and odd" Africans, who had been seized from a Portuguese slave ship en route to Spanish America. Some of the Africans were transported to Jamestown shortly thereafter. By 1625 at least nine African men and women lived here. Many of the colony's early Africans were held as slaves, but some individuals became free. A legal framework for hereditary, lifelong slavery evolved in Virginia during the 1600s. The United States abolished slavery in 1865.

V-47 HOT WATER/CENTERVILLE

At intersection of Centerville Road (Rte. 614) and Hot Water Road/Freedom Park. Royal Governor William Berkeley, owner of nearby Green Spring plantation, purchased the land here by 1652, then known as Hot Water. After Berkeley's death, the Hot Water tract passed to the Ludwell and Lee families. William Ludwell Lee inherited the property in 1796 and died in 1803. Lee's will specified that his slaves be freed when they reached the age of 18. They were allowed to live on the property for ten years at no charge and "comfortable houses" were to be built upon the tract for them. Lee's philanthropy gave rise to one of Virginia's early free black settlements located at Centerville.

KING WILLIAM COUNTY

O-18-a KING WILLIAM TRAINING SCHOOL

On King William Road (Rte. 30) approximately 500 feet east of intersection with Acquinton Church Road (Rte. 629). King William Training School was erected here in 1922–23 on the site of the King William Academy (1903–22). The Rosenwald Foundation, which built more than 5,300 black schools in the South, the African American community, and the county funded this school. Constructed as a Rosenwald Foundation Plan 4A building, it has natural lighting, four classrooms with a fifth added in 1927, and an auditorium, library, and office. The school provided a formal education in grades one through twelve. It served as a high school until 1952 and an elementary school until 1961. The Pamunkey Baptist Association bought the King William Training School in 1962.

OC-45 MT. NEBO BAPTIST CHURCH

In West Point at 1224 Kirby Street. African Americans held worship services in a nearby railroad toolshed during the Civil War. Jesse Dungee, later a member of the Virginia House of Delegates, organized the congregation (now known as Mt. Nebo) in 1866. The Gothic Revival-style sanctuary was built in 1887. During a boycott of West Point's segregated schools in 1952, attorney Oliver W. Hill told a large audience here that challenging the separate-but-equal doctrine was "worth going to jail for." Eight parents were later convicted of violating Virginia's compulsory school attendance law. In 1957 the Virginia Supreme Court of Appeals ruled in *Dobbins v. Commonwealth* that this application of the law was unconstitutional.

MATHEWS COUNTY

ND-17 THOMAS HUNTER (ROSENWALD) SCHOOL

In Mathews at 387 Church Street. African Americans formed the Mathews Educational League in 1923 and raised $9,900 to build a four-room school here in 1926-1927. Donations came mainly from the black community, with additional contributions from white residents, the county school board, and the Julius Rosenwald Fund. This fund, established by the president of Sears, Roebuck, and Co., and inspired by the work of Booker T. Washington, helped build more than 5,000 schools and supporting structures for black students between 1917 and 1932. Named for Thomas Hunter, a former slave, this school was accredited during the 1939-1940 session and moved into a new brick building here in 1953. County schools were desegregated in 1969.

MIDDLESEX COUNTY

OC-44 MORGAN V. VIRGINIA

In Saluda at intersection of General Puller Highway (Rte. 33) and New Street. Irene Morgan's resistance to segregation led to an important court case. On 16 July 1944, Morgan refused to give up her seat on a Greyhound bus to a white passenger. After a struggle with Middlesex County sheriffs she was arrested. Convicted by the State, she appealed all the way to the United States Supreme Court with the help of Spottswood W. Robinson III and Thurgood Marshall, among others. In a landmark decision in 1946, the Court ruled that it was unconstitutional to enforce segregation laws on interstate carriers. This decision helped set precedent for the later battles the NAACP waged against segregation.

OC-46 St. Clare Walker High School

At 2911 General Puller Highway (Rte. 33).
African American residents of Middlesex
County established the Langston Training School (later the Middlesex Training
School) in 1917 to serve elementary
and high school students. The Rosenwald Fund supported construction of a
new building ca. 1921. John Henry St.
Clare Walker, principal for two decades,
expanded the high school curriculum
from two to four years despite inadequate
funding. The high school moved here in
1939. Later renamed in Walker's honor, it
was among the first rural high schools for
black students to be accredited by the Virginia Department of Education. Students
garnered awards for academics, athletics,
and the arts. The county's school system
was desegregated in 1969.

NEW KENT COUNTY

WO-38 Green v. County School Board of New Kent County

*At 6501 New Kent Highway (Rte. 249) at
George W. Watkins Elementary School.*
In the 1968 *Green v. County School Board
of New Kent County* decision, the Supreme
Court of the United States abandoned the
"all deliberate speed" mandate of *Brown II*
(1955) and demanded immediate integration of schools. Black plaintiffs in New
Kent County had filed suit in 1965 with
assistance from the National Association
for the Advancement of Colored People
(NAACP). New Kent County maintained
two school systems despite the federal
mandate; black students attended Watkins
School, while white students attended
New Kent School. After *Green*, integrated
schools were defined not only by their
student bodies, but also by their faculties
and staffs.

WO-17 James Lafayette

At 12003 New Kent Highway (Rte. 249).
James Lafayette was born in slavery
about 1748 near here. His master William Armistead was commissary of military supplies when in the summer of
1781 the Marquis de Lafayette recruited
James as a spy. Posing as a double agent,
forager, and servant at British headquarters, James moved freely between
the lines with vital information on British troop movements for Lafayette. The
Virginia General Assembly freed James
in 1787 in recognition of his bravery
and service, on the written recommen-
dation of Lafayette, whose name he
took for his own. He died in Baltimore
on 9 Aug. 1830.

CITY OF NEWPORT NEWS

W-68   Camp Hill and Camp Alexander

*Marker currently missing. Recasting pend-
ing.* Camps Hill and Alexander were created when Newport News was designated
a port of embarkation by the U.S. Army
after the United States entered World
War I in 1917. Camp Hill was established
in Aug. 1917 and named for Confederate
Lt. Gen. A. P. Hill. Besides processing
men for overseas duty, it served as the
port's animal embarkation area. Camp
Alexander was established in 1918 and
served as an embarkation and postwar
debarkation camp for African American
troops. It was named for Lt. John Hank
Alexander, one of the first African American graduates of West Point. After World
War I, the camps were abandoned.

W-70-a Ella Fitzgerald (1917–1996)

*At intersection of 26th Street (Rte. 60) and
Madison Avenue.*   Born here in Newport News 25 Apr. 1917, Ella Fitzgerald,
known as Lady Ella or the First Lady of

Song, was considered one of the most influential jazz vocalists of the 20th century. Her three-octave vocal range and improvisational ability in scat singing won her recognition worldwide. Fitzgerald's first hit, "A-Tisket, A-Tasket," was recorded in 1938. She later recorded eight critically acclaimed "Songbook" albums, her most commercially successful work. The winner of 13 Grammys and a recipient of the National Medal of Art and the Presidential Medal of Freedom, among other honors, Fitzgerald died in Beverly Hills, California, 15 June 1996.

W-102 GEORGE W. CARVER HIGH SCHOOL

At 6158 Jefferson Avenue (Rte. 17). African American residents of Warwick County campaigned for new public schools to replace inadequate, overcrowded facilities in the 1930s and 1940s. In 1949 the county opened Carver High School, constructed here at a cost of more than $500,000. The 20-classroom consolidated school served students in grades 1-11, with grade 12 added in 1955. In July 1958 Carver was incorporated into the Newport News school system. Homer L. Hines, the school's only principal, inspired students to high achievement. Carver High School closed in 1971 as part of the city's desegregation plan, and the building became an intermediate school.

W-77 JAMES A. FIELDS HOUSE

On 27th Street between Jefferson and Madison Avenues. James A. Fields acquired this late-Victorian Italianate-style brick house in 1893. Fields, born into slavery in Hanover County, escaped in 1862 and became a contraband of war. He graduated in 1871 from what is now Hampton University and taught school. After receiving a law degree from Howard University in 1882, Fields served as the commonwealth's attorney for Warwick County in 1887 and represented the region in the House of Delegates (1889-1890). After Field's death in 1903, four doctors acquired the house in 1908 and it functioned as Newport News' first black hospital. Eventually the hospital became known as Whittaker Memorial Hospital at another site.

W-78 JESSIE MENIFIELD RATTLEY

At 2901 Jefferson Avenue (Rte. 143). Educator, politician, and Civil Rights pioneer, Jessie Menifield Rattley (1929–2001) was born in Birmingham, Alabama. She graduated from Hampton University in 1951. Rattley founded the Peninsula Business College here in 1952. She was the first black woman elected to the Newport News City Council and served from 1970 until 1990. In 1986 she became the city's first black and female mayor. Rattley was the first black president of the Virginia Municipal League (1978–1979) and in 1979 was elected the first black woman president of the National League of Cities. Rattley also served on a number of commissions, delegations, and taskforces for the U.S. government and other organizations.

W-172 PEARL BAILEY (1918–1990)

At intersection of Chestnut Avenue and 29th Street. Pearl Bailey, singer, author, and humanitarian, was born in Newport News. Her family, including brother Willie "Bill" Bailey, a famous tap dancer, lived at 1204 and later at 1202 29th St. For five decades, beginning in the 1930s, she performed in nightclubs, on Broadway, in movies, and on television, captivating audiences with her distinctive voice and humorous asides. Bailey received a special Tony Award in 1968 for her starring role in *Hello, Dolly!* For many years she toured with the USO to enter-

Pearl Bailey. Marker W-172. (William Morris Agency, Creative Commons)

tain American troops. During the 1970s and 1980s, she served as a U.S. representative to the General Assembly of the United Nations. Bailey was awarded the Presidential Medal of Freedom in 1988.

CITY OF NORFOLK

KN-3 BANK STREET BAPTIST CHURCH

At intersection of E. Charlotte Street and St. Paul's Boulevard. The Bank Street Baptist Church was built on this site in 1802 as a Presbyterian church. In 1840 it was purchased by a group of free blacks to serve them as a Baptist church. Because it had one of the first church bells in Norfolk, the building was known as the Bell Church. The church continued to serve the black community until its demolition in 1967 when the congregation moved to its new location on Chesapeake Boulevard.

KV-30 BOOKER T. WASHINGTON HIGH SCHOOL

At 1111 Park Avenue (Rte. 58). John T. West High School, one of Virginia's first accredited public high schools for African Americans, was renamed in 1917 for Booker T. Washington, educator, author, and orator. The school moved to a newly constructed building in 1924 and for decades was Norfolk's only public high school for black students. Its programs were central to the community. In 1939-1940, faculty members Aline Black and Melvin Alston pursued legal action that led to a federal court decision requiring salary equalization for black and white teachers. In Sept. 1963, students marched to protest poor facilities. Norfolk implemented a desegregation plan in 1970, and the school moved into a new building here in 1974.

KV-20 ELLA J. BAKER (1903–1986)

On Church Street (Rte. 460) at intersection with Brickhouse Avenue. Ella Baker, born in Norfolk, was a leader in the Civil Rights Movement for five decades. In the 1940s she was a field secretary with the National Association for the Advancement of Colored People and later served as its director of branches. Baker helped to establish the Southern Christian Leadership Conference in 1957 working alongside Dr. Martin Luther King, Jr. In 1960 she helped to launch the Student Nonviolent Coordinating Committee, and she served as mentor to a generation of young activists. A strong proponent of grassroots leadership, Baker believed: "Give people light and they will find a way."

KV-16 NAVY MESS ATTENDANT SCHOOL

At intersection of Bacon Avenue and Morris Street, aboard Naval Station Norfolk. From 1933 to 1942, Navy recruits of African descent attended this school, located in barracks at Unit "K-West" and later at

"B-East." Advancement opportunities for these sailors and counterparts of Asian Pacific Island heritage were then limited to serving as officer's cooks or stewards. The school moved to Unit "X" in 1942 before training was relocated to Bainbridge, Maryland, and elsewhere. Though racial segregation continued, all job ratings were re-opened to qualified personnel in 1942. Mess attendants were re-designated "steward's mates" in 1943, and more than 1,100 members of the messman/steward branch were killed during World War II. Norfolk trainees decorated for heroism include Navy Cross recipients Doris Miller, William Pinckney, and Leonard Harmon.

WY-20 PLUMMER BERNARD YOUNG SR. (1884–1962)

On Church Street between E. Olney Road and Nicholson Street.   North Carolina native Plummer Bernard (P. B.) Young moved to Norfolk in 1907 to work at the *Lodge Journal and Guide*, the newspaper of an African American fraternal organization. He bought the paper in 1910, expanded its scope, and renamed it the *Journal and Guide*. By the 1940s, it was among the most widely circulated African American weeklies in the nation, and Young became one of Virginia's most influential black citizens. His newspaper championed racial equality, urging better housing, schools, jobs, and municipal services for African Americans. Young, a trustee of Howard University and Hampton Institute, also chaired the advisory board of what is now Norfolk State University.

KV-25 WEST POINT CEMETERY

On E. Princess Anne Road between Salter Street and Armistead Avenue.   This historically African American burial place, first known as Potter's Field, was established as Calvary Cemetery in 1873 and renamed West Point Cemetery in 1885.

James E. Fuller, Norfolk's first African American councilman, secured a section for the burial of black Union Civil War veterans in 1886. Nearly 60 soldiers and sailors were interred there. Fuller led efforts to mark the site with a monument, completed in 1920, that honors African Americans who served in the Civil War and the Spanish-American War. At its top is a statue of Sgt. William H. Carney, Norfolk native and the first black Medal of Honor recipient. West Point Cemetery is listed on the National Register of Historic Places.

NORTHAMPTON COUNTY

WY-73 CAPE CHARLES COLORED SCHOOL

In Cape Charles on Old Cape Charles Road (Rte. 641) approximately 2000 feet south of Mason Avenue.   Constructed in 1928, this school opened about 1930 for African American children in Cape Charles during legalized segregation. The building was constructed with contributions from the local African American community, the State Literary Fund, and the Julius Rosenwald Fund, established in 1917 to build schools for African American students in the rural South. Staffed by three teachers and a principal/teacher, the school housed grades one through seven, and was a center for educational, social, and cultural events for the African American community. Under Principal Jesse L. Hare, the school closed in 1966 when Northampton County Schools were consolidated four years before their integration.

WY-72 NORTHAMPTON COUNTY HIGH SCHOOL

On Young Street (Rte. 627), 800 feet west of Lankford Highway (Rte. 13). Constructed in 1953 as the county's first purpose-built African American

Migratory agricultural workers on board the Princess Anne going to the Eastern Shore of Virginia, July 1940. (New York Public Library Digital Collections)

high school, Northampton County High School reflects the desires of local African Americans to obtain modern educational facilities. It is an example of the statewide efforts by African American and Virginia Indian communities during the early 20th century to secure better education for their children. The building contained classrooms, a library, a gymnasium, and a 500-seat auditorium. Concurrent with integration of Virginia's public schools, the high school ceased operations with the 1970 class. Until 2008, the facility served as a junior high school and middle school for all Northampton County students.

WY-11-a   PETER JACOB CARTER

At 7638 Bayside Road.   Born enslaved on 29 May 1845 near Eastville, Northampton County, Peter Jacob Carter served in the 10th United States Colored Troops during the Civil War and afterward attended Hampton Institute. He represented Northampton in the House of Delegates from 1871 to 1879, was conspicuous in First Congressional District politics, chaired Republican state conventions and African American mass meetings, and

attended the party's national conventions. A prominent Eastern Shore politician, in the 1880s he joined the Readjuster Party, led by former Confederate general William Mahone. Carter died 19 July 1886 and was buried in the family cemetery near Franktown.

WY-2   SITE OF TIDEWATER INSTITUTE

On Cobbs Station Road (Rte. 636) approximately 4000 feet east of Lankford Highway (Rte. 13).   Tidewater Institute was incorporated in 1903 with the stated purpose of establishing an industrial, academic, collegiate, and seminary boarding school for the education of black youth. Founded by the Rev. George E. Reid, and supported by the Northampton/Accomack Baptist Association, the institute attracted students from both Virginia and other Atlantic seaboard states. For twenty-eight years, the school was dedicated to the education and molding of lives of young black men and women of Virginia's Eastern Shore.

CITY OF PORTSMOUTH

Q-8-t EMANUEL A.M.E. CHURCH

At intersection of Green and North Streets.
Emanuel A.M.E. Church is rooted in
the African Methodist Society that was
formed soon after the founding in 1772
of the Methodist Society in Portsmouth.
The African Society met independently
until Nat Turner's Insurrection in 1831,
worshiped with white Methodists for
three years, then met under white super-
vision until 1864. The members occupied
a Methodist church on Glasgow Street
until the building burned in 1856. Slaves
and free blacks provided most of the
funds and labor to construct North Street
Methodist Church in 1857. In 1871, the
congregation adopted the name Emanuel
("God with us") and became part of the
African Methodist Episcopal movement.

Q-8-x GEORGE TEAMOH

*At the intersection of Queen and Green
Streets.* A member of the Constitutional
Convention of 1867 and the Senate of
Virginia from 1869 until 1871, George
Teamoh was born enslaved in Portsmouth
where he spent most of his early life.
A skilled laborer, he served as a ship's
carpenter and caulker in the Tidewater
area. After his family was sold away from
him, he escaped from slavery in 1853 by
jumping ship in New York while hired
out on a mercantile voyage. He resided in
Massachusetts until the end of the Civil
War when he returned to Portsmouth and
became an important community leader.
Teamoh died sometime after 1883.

Q-81   ISRAEL CHARLES NORCOM HIGH
SCHOOL

At 1801 London Boulevard (Rte. 141).
I. C. Norcom (1856-1916) was an African
American educator and administrator

who served Portsmouth schools for more
than 30 years. The first school to bear
his name opened in 1920 three quarters
of a mile southeast of here. Principal
William E. Riddick and vice principal
Lavinia M. Weaver led it for decades. The
school moved into a new building nearby
in 1937 and again relocated to a new
facility, about a mile southwest of here,
in 1953. The school's academic, athletic,
and cultural programs were central to the
community. Students conducted sit-ins to
desegregate Portsmouth lunch counters
in 1960, and alumni became local, state,
and national leaders. Norcom High
School moved here in 1998.

Q-8-w MATILDA SISSIERETTA JOYNER
JONES   (1869–1933)

At intersection of Green and North Streets.
Born Matilda S. Joyner in Portsmouth
1869, Sissieretta Jones was a trailblazing
African American pioneer of the concert
and theatrical stages during the late 19th
and early 20th centuries. She studied
music at the Providence School of Music
and the New England Conservatory
in Boston. Jones sang for several U.S.
presidents and at the Chicago world's
fair in 1893. While performing with the
"Black Patti Troubadours" she always
closed each show with brilliant renditions
of opera and gospel music. Her popularity spanned the globe, and she received
medals and lavish gifts from many foreign
heads of state.

Q-8-z MOUNT CALVARY CEMETERY
COMPLEX

*On Pulaski Street approximately 400 feet
west of Deep Creek Boulevard.*   African Americans purchased land about a
quarter mile southwest of here in 1879
to establish Mt. Olive Cemetery. The
property adjoins a potter's field thought
to be a burial place for victims of the

Portrait photograph of Sissieretta Jones by Napoleon Sarony, c. 1895. Marker Q-8-w. (National Portrait Gallery)

yellow fever epidemic of 1855. Later, Mt. Calvary and Fishers Hill Cemeteries were founded nearby, creating a four-cemetery complex. Buried there are many community leaders, including Baptist minister John M. Armistead, educators Ida Barbour and I. C. Norcom, and journalist Jeffrey T. Wilson. Also interred there are formerly enslaved persons, Civil War-era U.S. Colored Troops, late-19th-century elected officials, and veterans of World Wars I and II.

Q-8-u RUTH BROWN (1928–2006)

At intersection of Green and North Streets. Portsmouth native Ruth Brown was the best-selling African American female recording artist early in the 1950s. Her two dozen hits established Atlantic Records as "The House That Ruth Built." Brown also helped to usher in the rock'n'roll genre during the 1950s when promoter Alan Freed introduced America to her vocal style in 1956. She enjoyed her first crossover hit, "Lucky Lips," in 1957. Among other honors, she won a Tony Award for her performance in the musical Black and Blue in 1989. Brown was inducted into the Rock and Roll Hall of Fame in 1993 as "the Queen Mother of the Blues."

SOUTHAMPTON COUNTY

U-120-a Benjamin F. Hicks (1847–1925)

At intersection of Ivor Road (Rte. 616) and St. Lukes Road (Rte. 633). Born six miles north of here near Courtland in the Berlin-Ivor District of Southampton County, African American Benjamin Hicks made his living by farming. Highly respected for his industrious and creative talents, he used the anvil, forge, and woodworking devices in his machine shop to improve peanut farming methods. By 1902, Hicks had received a patent for his invention of a gasoline-powered machine for stemming and cleaning peanuts and is noted for his contributions to the development of the peanut harvester. Hick's picker is believed to have helped revolutionize farming in Southampton and the peanut growing area. He is buried on his farm.

U-115 Buckhorn (Ridley's) Quarter

At intersection of Southampton Parkway (Rte. 58) and Buckhorn Quarter Road. On 21 Aug. 1831, enslaved preacher Nat Turner launched a revolt that resulted in the deaths of about 60 whites and a similar number of African Americans. Defeated in a skirmish outside Jerusalem (now Courtland) on 22 Aug., the rebels came to this neighborhood, site of some of the largest slaveholdings in the area. They spent the night at Maj. Thomas Ridley's Buckhorn Quarter plantation, about a mile north of here. Local whites seeking refuge spent the night elsewhere on Ridley's property. Four of Ridley's slaves joined the revolt, but other participants deserted amid fears of a white attack. The rebels left before dawn on 23 Aug. and were defeated later that day, ending the revolt.

U-55 Courtland School—Rosenwald Funded

In Courtland at 25499 Florence Street. Courtland School, which served African American students during the segregation era, was erected here in 1928-29 at a cost of $4,000. The local African American community raised $1,000, while the county contributed $2,500. The Julius Rosenwald Fund, established by the president of Sears, Roebuck and Company, contributed $500. Rosenwald's program, which helped pay for the construction of more than 5,000 schools for African Americans across the rural South between 1917 and 1932, was inspired by the work of Booker T. Washington, who died in 1915. Courtland School, built on a stan-

A map of the area in which Nat Turner's Insurrection took place. Courtland, the county seat for Southampton County, was originally named Jerusalem. Marker U-122. (Gilmer map, Library of Congress)

Booker T. Washington. Markers U-58, KP-14, and KV-30. (New York Public Library Digital Collections)

dard two-teacher architectural plan, later became Courtland Community Center.

UT-24   DRED SCOTT AND THE BLOW FAMILY

At the intersection of Southampton Parkway (Rte. 58) and Buckhorn Quarter Road. Dred Scott, a slave, lived as a child northeast of here on the Peter Blow plantation early in the 1800s. The Blows moved to Missouri and in 1830 sold Scott to an army officer who was stationed in various free territories. Scott sued for his and his family's freedom in 1846 because he lived where slavery was illegal. In 1857, however, the U.S. Supreme Court ruled that Congress could not outlaw slavery and that Scott was property, not a citizen. The Dred Scott decision outraged abolitionists and further divided the nation. Blow's sons purchased Scott's freedom in 1857; he died in 1858.

U-122   NAT TURNER'S INSURRECTION

On Meherrin Road (Rte. 35) approximately 600 feet south of Cross Keys Road. On the night of 21-22 August 1831, Nat Turner, a slave preacher, began an insurrection some seven miles west with a band that grew to about 70. They moved northeast toward the Southampton County seat, Jerusalem (now Courtland), killing about 60 whites. After two days militiamen and armed civilians quelled the revolt. Turner was captured on 30 October, tried and convicted, and hanged on 11 November; some 30 blacks were hanged or expelled from Virginia. In response to the revolt, the General Assembly passed harsher slave laws and censored abolitionists.

CITY OF SUFFOLK

K-322   AFRICAN AMERICAN OYSTERMEN

Opposite 8300 Crittenden Road (Rte. 628). Hobson is an example of an African American oystering village that developed during the last quarter of the 19th century on the James River, the Chesapeake Bay and their tributaries. As in other watermen communities, people also farmed and worked at nearby shucking houses and canning facilities. Hobson's black oystermen worked oyster beds in the James and Nansemond Rivers and Chuckatuck Creek that were leased primarily from the state. Bay region oyster beds were once among the richest in the world. Starting in the late 1950s Virginia's oyster production declined because of pollution, such as the chemical kepone, oyster diseases, weather, and over-harvesting, which caused many of the oystermen to leave in the search of other employment.

U-58 BOOKER T. WASHINGTON HIGH SCHOOL

On Smith Street at the intersection with Lee Street. The Suffolk School Board opened Booker T. Washington School here in 1913 to serve African American children in grades 1-8. Ninth grade was added during the 1920s. Overcrowding prompted the construction of a larger building here in 1925. Black residents successfully campaigned for the addition of a senior high curriculum, and the first high school class graduated in 1937. Administrator J. F. Peele Jr. provided leadership for four decades. Again overcrowded, the school relocated to a new building one and a half miles east in 1953. The last high school class graduated in 1969. Washington became an intermediate school and later an elementary school.

K-332 EAST SUFFOLK SCHOOL COMPLEX

At 134 S. 6th Street. Between 1926 and 1927, African Americans raised $3,300 toward the East Suffolk School, which opened with T. J. Johnson as principal. In addition to public money, the Julius Rosenwald Fund also provided $1,500 to assist the effort. Rosenwald, president of Sears, Roebuck & Company, established the fund in 1917 and helped pay for the construction of more than 5,000 schools for African Americans in 15 southern states. In 1939, at the request of the local community, the Works Progress Administration's "Pump Priming Program" funded the addition of the County Training School, later known as East Suffolk High School, with the first class graduating in 1940. The last class graduated in 1965.

K-271 FLORENCE GRADED SCHOOL

At 4540 Nansemond Parkway (Rte. 337). Florence Graded School was named for Florence Bowser, a noted educator who taught here and was instrumental in having the school constructed. It was built in 1920 with state and local funds and a grant from the Julius Rosenwald Fund, which had been created about 1912 to finance elementary schools for rural southern African Americans. Some 5,000 Rosenwald schools were built in 15 states, including 308 in Virginia; 9 were in Suffolk (then Nansemond County). Elements of the original frame building survive in the present brick structure. The adjoining Florence Bowser Elementary School was completed in 1963.

K-333 HUNTERSVILLE ROSENWALD SCHOOL

On Hunters Court at the intersection with Hampton Roads Parkway. The Huntersville School was built in 1930-31 as a Rosenwald School. The Julius Rosenwald fund provided $1,000 toward the construction, with contributions from African Americans and the local government provided the rest of its $7,000 cost. Rosenwald, president of Sears, Roebuck & Company, established the fund in 1917 and helped pay for the construction of more than 5,000 schools for African Americans in 15 southern states. The Huntersville School was one of the last built in Virginia, as the program ended in 1932. It included classroom space for four teachers and was named for its first principal, Joseph S. Gibson.

K-310 JAMES BOWSER, REVOLUTIONARY SOLDIER

On Nansemond Highway (Rte. 337) at Driver Lane.   James Bowser, a free African American born in Nansemond County about 1763, was one of many black Virginians who served in the army or navy of the United States during the Revolutionary War. He enlisted in the 1st Virginia Regiment of the Continental Line under Col. William Davies on 1 Jan. 1782 in Shenandoah County for the duration of the war. After the war ended in 1783, he returned to Nansemond County, where he lived nearby, married, and reared a large family of freeborn citizens. For his service to his country, Bowser's heirs were granted a bounty land warrant in 1834.

U-129 MOUNT SINAI BAPTIST CHURCH

At 6100 Holy Neck Road.   In 1868, the formerly enslaved Rev. Israel Cross founded Mount Sinai Baptist Church in a log building here on Benjamin Howell's land. He allegedly never closed a sermon without saying, "Buy some land, build a home, and get some education." In 1871, the congregation replaced the log church with a wood-frame building, later remodeled in 1908 and 1911. The current Gothic Revival building was constructed in 1921. Carter G. Woodson, author of *The Rural Negro* (1930 edition), called it "An Unusual Church for the Rural Community." Annexes were added to the church in 1966 and 2000.

KO-2 NANSEMOND COLLEGIATE INSTITUTE

On E. Washington Street (Rte. 13 Bus.) between N. 4th and N. 5th Streets.   Here stood the Nansemond Collegiate Insti-tute, founded in 1890 as the Nansemond Industrial Institute by Rev. William W. Gaines to provide local black children with an education, because free public schools were closed to them. Eventually the institute offered elementary, second-ary, and normal school courses of instruc-tion. In 1927 a public school for black students was opened; competition for students and a series of disastrous fires forced the institute to close in 1939.

U-128 NANSEMOND COUNTY TRAINING SCHOOL

At intersection of S. Quay Road (Rte. 58) and Leafwood Road.   Two miles south stood the Nansemond County Training School, the first high school in the county for African American students. It was constructed in 1924 with $5,000 con-tributed by African American families, $11,500 in public money, and $1,500 from the Rosenwald Fund, established in 1917 to build schools for African Amer-ican students in the rural South. The building, with seven classrooms and one auditorium, contained an elementary and secondary school. Hannibal E. Howell was its first principal, serving for 42 years. In 1964, the name was changed to Southwestern High School and after the racial integration of county schools, be-came Southwestern Intermediate School.

K-163 OAK LAWN CEMETERY

At 449 Market Street.   Seven African American trustees acquired land here in 1885 and established Oak Lawn Ceme-tery. Community leaders interred here include John W. Richardson, president of the Phoenix Bank of Nansemond; Wiley H. Crocker, founder of the Tidewater Fair Association and Nansemond Develop-ment Corporation; William W. Gaines, Baptist minister and founder of the Nansemond Collegiate Institute; Fletcher Mae Howell, Baptist missionary; Dr. Wil-liam T. Fuller, physician and banker; and William H. Walker, Tuskegee Airman. Also buried here are late-19th-century local politicians, United States Colored Troops, and veterans of World Wars I and II, Korea, and Vietnam.

SURRY COUNTY

K-320 Jerusalem Baptist Church

At 6512 Carsley Road (Rte. 615). Jerusalem Baptist Church was organized as Mt. Joy Baptist Church in 1867 at the nearby home of Mondoza Bailey, community leader and carpenter. Amelia "Mother" Howard assisted in the organization of this and six other churches. Sent by the United States Freedmen's Bureau, Howard, a teacher from Pennsylvania, helped to establish African American schools and churches in the region. Bailey led church members in the construction of a wooden building. Nancy Ellis James, born a free African American woman, and her family provided the land here for the church. The current brick structure was built in 1993.

K-331 Temperance Industrial & Collegiate Institute

On Colonial Trail West (Rte. 10) at intersection with Martin Luther King Highway (Rte. 40). On 12 Oct. 1892, Dr. John Jefferson Smallwood, born enslaved in 1863 in Rich Square, North Carolina, founded the Temperance Industrial & Collegiate Institute nearby with fewer than ten students. Sprawled over sixty-five acres on the James River in Claremont, his school provided a high level of education for African American boys and girls from Virginia and other states. After Smallwood's untimely death on 29 Sept. 1912, his school underwent several mergers and name changes. By the time the school closed in 1928, more than two thousand students had attended.

SUSSEX COUNTY

UO-8 Hunting Quarter Baptist Church

At 16166 Hunting Quarter Church Road (Rte. 662). Hunting Quarter Baptist Church originated ca. 1863 when local African Americans began holding worship services under a nearby brush arbor, according to oral history. White neighbors donated a two-room sanctuary that stood 200 feet northeast of here and burned in 1865. The congregation built a frame sanctuary here in 1879 and later overlaid it with brick. During the segregation era, the church supported Hunting Quarter School for African American children. Buried in the cemetery is longtime pastor Frank L. Mason, Republican candidate for U.S. Congress from Virginia's 4th District in 1920. Also interred here are veterans of World Wars I and II.

CITY OF VIRGINIA BEACH

KV-15-a Civilian Conservation Corps Company 1371

At First Landing State Park Visitor Center, 2500 Shore Drive (Rte. 60). Seashore State Park at Cape Henry, now known as First Landing State Park, was built by an all African American regiment of the Civilian Conservation Corps, a New Deal–era relief program that employed young men ages 17 to 25. The CCC program provided food, clothing, medical care, and educational opportunities for men caught in the financial turmoil of the Great Depression. Company 1371 constructed more than 20 miles of trails, drained the marsh, built cabins, and planted a wide variety of trees and shrubs. In 1944, the CCC disbanded in response to recruitment efforts for WWII.

Ella Fitzgerald with Dizzy Gillespie, Ray Brown, Milt (Milton) Jackson, and Timmie Rosenkrantz at the Downbeat, New York, c. 1947. Markers W-70-a, and W-107. (Library of Congress)

K-274 PRINCESS ANNE COUNTY TRAIN-ING SCHOOL/UNION KEMPSVILLE HIGH SCHOOL

At 5100 Cleveland Street. This is the site of Princess Anne County Training School, the first school for African Americans in the county. The Princess Anne County Training Association and surrounding communities raised money to purchase property to build a high school. In 1934 a temporary site was established at Union Baptist Church until a four-room building was completed in 1938. The high school later expanded in size and faculty and was renamed Union Kempsville High in 1961, just before the county became the city of Virginia Beach. In 1969 the high school closed after citywide racial integration made it necessary. The last class graduated in 1969.

KV-32 SGT. MILES JAMES (CA. 1829–CA. 1871)

Dedication pending. Location pending. Miles James, born into slavery in Princess Anne County, made his way to Portsmouth and enlisted in the U.S. Army in Nov. 1863. He was mustered into service at Fort Monroe and soon became a corporal in the 36th U.S. Colored Infantry. James was awarded the Medal of Honor for extraordinary heroism in action at New Market Heights, VA, on 29 Sept. 1864. After a bullet shattered his arm, necessitating an immediate field amputation, he continued to fight and urged his men forward within 30 yards of the Confederate works. Promoted to sergeant, he returned to duty by April 1865. He served briefly in Texas before rejoining his family in Norfolk. James died ca. 1871 of complications from his wound.

CITY OF WILLIAMSBURG

W-108 First Baptist Church

At 727 Scotland Street.   This church, home to one of the oldest continuous congregations organized by African Americans, traces its origins to brush arbor meetings held by 1776 at a nearby plantation. The congregation moved to a Williamsburg carriage house and in 1856 completed a brick sanctuary on Nassau Street. A school for black students opened there in the 1860s. The Rev. John Dawson, longtime pastor, served in the Senate of Virginia from 1874 to 1877. First Baptist moved into its sanctuary here in 1956. During the Civil Rights era, the Rev. David Collins led demonstrations for fair hiring practices and joined the Southern Christian Leadership Conference. Dr. Martin Luther King, Jr. spoke here in 1962.

W-109   School for Black Children

At 107 N. Boundary Street.   The Associates of Dr. Bray, a London-based charity, founded a school for enslaved and free black children here in 1760. Located in Williamsburg at the suggestion of Benjamin Franklin, a member of the Associates, the school received support from the College of William & Mary. Anne Wager instructed as many as 400 boys and girls during her 14 years as teacher. In a culture hostile to educating African Americans, Wager taught the students principles of Christianity, deportment, reading, and, possibly, writing. The curriculum reinforced proslavery ideology but also spread literacy within the black community. The school moved from this site by 1765 and closed in 1774.

YORK COUNTY

NP-13   Mary Aggie and the Benefit of Clergy

On Goosley Road (Rte. 238), 300 feet east of George Washington Memorial Highway (Rte. 17).   Mary Aggie, an enslaved woman, was convicted of theft in York County in 1730. Lt. Gov. William Gooch impressed with Mary's profession of faith when she had sued previously for her freedom, supported her 1730 claim for "benefit of clergy," which then allowed only white men to escape the harshest penalties for most first offenses by reading a passage from the Bible. Gooch's support resulted in Aggie's pardon. In 1732, the General Assembly extended a limited form of benefit of clergy to all races and to women. Aggie was sold out of Virginia in 1731, probably never knowing her appeal's significant legal effect. Virginia abolished the benefit by 1848.

Dr. Martin Luther King, Jr. speaks with members of First Baptist Church in Williamsburg, June 1962. Marker W-108. (Photo courtesy First Baptist Church)

Black students seek to reopen their schools closed by Prince Edward County authorities. Farmville, Virginia. July 1963. (Robert Russa Moton Museum)

REGION FIVE

Southern Piedmont, Blue Ridge, and Southwest

Appomattox County

Brunswick County

Buckingham County

Cumberland County

City of Danville

City of Emporia

Franklin County

Halifax County

Lunenburg County

City of Lynchburg

City of Martinsville

Mecklenburg County

Montgomery County

Nottoway County

Prince Edward County

City of Radford

City of Roanoke

Wise County

Wythe County

APPOMATTOX COUNTY

M-37   AFRICAN AMERICAN BANJOISTS

On Old Court House Road (Rte. 24) approximately one mile east of entrance to Appomattox Court House National Historic Park.   West Africans developed the forerunners of the modern banjo. Free and enslaved Africans in the Americas later made similar stringed instruments, typically of animal hides, gourds, wood, and gut or horsehair. Black musicians who lived near here, whose identities are now unknown, taught the banjo to Joel Walker Sweeney (ca. 1810-1860), a local white musician who brought international fame to the banjo and himself. The banjo, in modified form, became a mainstay of American popular culture by the end of the 19th century. By drawing on their musical traditions, this region's African American banjoists shaped the diverse world of American music.

BRUNSWICK COUNTY

S-92   NELLIE PRATT RUSSELL
(1890–1979)

On Christanna Highway (Rte. 46) approximately 280 feet east of the intersection with Boydton Plank Road (Rte. 1).   Nellie Pratt Russell, educator, attended Howard University and was one of six incorporators of Alpha Kappa Alpha Sorority, the first Greek letter organization founded by African American women. The sorority, established in 1908, was incorporated in Jan. 1913, preserving its traditions and securing its right to charter new chapters. In 1931 Russell earned a Master of Arts degree from Teachers College, Columbia University. For about 50 years, she taught English at the Saint Paul Normal and Industrial School (later Saint Paul's College), where she helped found Gamma Lambda Omega chapter of Alpha Kappa Alpha.

Russell led women's organizations in the Episcopal Diocese of Southern Virginia.

SN-67   SAINT PAUL'S CHAPEL SCHOOL—
ROSENWALD FUNDED

On Brunswick Drive (Rte. 644) between Interstate 85 and Shining Creek Road (Rte. 619).   Among the earliest of the more than a dozen Julius Rosenwald Schools built in Brunswick County, Saint Paul's Chapel School was constructed as a one-teacher standard plan in 1920 under the initial wave of Tuskegee Institute-administered building funds. Contributors included the Rosenwald Fund ($300), local black families ($450), and public money ($750) for a total of $1,500. Between 1917 and 1932, the Rosenwald Fund helped build more than 5,000 African American schools across the rural South. Former student Erwin L. Avery restored the school in 2004. It is on the National Register of Historic Places and the Virginia Landmarks Register.

SN-63   SAINT PAUL'S COLLEGE

In Lawrenceville on N. Main Street (Rte. 58 Bus.) at the intersection with Athletic Field Road.   Saint Paul's College was established in 1883 by the Venerable James Solomon Russell (1857-1935) as an Episcopal mission school to serve the black community of Southside Virginia. Born into slavery in Mecklenburg County, Russell was educated at Hampton Institute and trained for the clergy at Bishop Payne Divinity School in Petersburg. His school was chartered in 1888 and incorporated as Saint Paul's Normal and Industrial School in 1890. Classes were held in the three-room Saul Building on the campus. The charter was amended in 1941, changing the school to a four-year, degree-granting college. Its name was changed to Saint Paul's College in 1957.

BUCKINGHAM COUNTY

F-62 BUCKINGHAM TRAINING SCHOOL

In Dillwyn on N. James Madison Highway (Rte. 15) at intersection with S. Constitution Route (Rte. 20). One mile southeast stood Buckingham Training School, the first high school in the county for African American students. In 1919 the Rev. Stephen J. Ellis organized the County-Wide League for School Improvement to persuade the Buckingham County School Board to build a secondary school for black students. When this effort failed, Ellis and his supporters raised $3,000 to match a grant from the Julius Rosenwald Fund, established in 1917 to build schools for black students in the rural South. The four-room high school opened in 1924 with Thomas L. Dabney as principal and served the community until it closed in 1953.

F-53 CARTER G. WOODSON (1875–1950)

At 27294 N. James Madison Highway (Rte. 15). Three miles east is the birthplace of the noted teacher, educator and historian, Dr. Carter G. Woodson. He was the founder of the Association for the Study of Negro Life and History, *Journal of Negro History*, originated Negro History Week and authored more than a dozen important works dealing with his race in the United States.

F-57 CARTER G. WOODSON BIRTHPLACE

On C. G. Woodson Road (Rte. 670) at intersection with N. James Madison Highway (Rte. 15). Carter Godwin Woodson was born about three miles east on 19 December 1875. As a youth he mined coal near Huntington, W.Va. He earned degrees at Berea College (B.L., 1903), University of Chicago (B.A. and M.A., 1908), and Harvard (Ph.D., 1912)—one of the first blacks awarded a doctorate by Harvard.

Carter G. Woodson. Markers F-53 and F-57. (AP Photo)

In 1915 he organized the Association for the Study of Negro Life and History and in 1916 established the *Journal of Negro History*. Known as the Father of Afro-American History, Woodson founded Negro History Week—now Afro-American History Month—in 1926. He died in Washington, D.C., on 3 April 1950.

CUMBERLAND COUNTY

O-55 JAMES F. LIPSCOMB

On Cumberland Road (Rte. 45) approximately 1100 feet north of Atkins Road (Rte. 701). James F. Lipscomb was born a free black on 4 December 1830 in Cumberland County. He worked first as a farm laborer, then as a carriage driver in Richmond. In 1867 he returned to Cumberland County, where he accumulated more than 500 acres of land. Lipscomb served in the House of Delegates between 1869 and 1877, one of 87 African-Americans elected to the General Assembly in the late 19th century. In 1871 he opened a general store in his home, part of which stands nearby, and operated it until his death on 10 August 1893. His grandson and granddaughter-in-law, John and Romaine Lipscomb, moved it into a new building on this site in 1921. The Lipscomb store, a community institution and social center, was closed in 1971 and demolished in 1987.

CITY OF DANVILLE

Q-5-m   BLOODY MONDAY

At 401 Patton Street. In the spring of 1963 local African American ministers and other leaders organized the Danville Movement to combat widespread racial segregation and discrimination. On 10 June, two demonstrations occurred. Police clubbed and fire-hosed the marchers, injuring at least 47 and arresting 60. The Rev. Dr. Martin Luther King, Jr., offered protesters his "full, personal support" when he arrived in Danville on 11 July. The nonviolent protests, which became known as "Bloody Monday," gained national news coverage before the 28 Aug. March on Washington co-led by the Rev. Dr. King. Both events swelled sentiment in favor of civil rights legislation.

Q-44   FIRST STATE BANK

At 201 N. Union Street. First State Bank, one of the few banks in Virginia owned by African Americans, opened on 8 Sept. 1919 as the Savings Bank of Danville. By issuing loans to individuals, businesses, and churches, the bank fostered the black community's vitality during the era of segregation. Maceo Conrad Martin (1897-1981), an officer of the bank from 1919 to 1970, became its president in 1951 and was later president of the National Bankers Association. The only black member of a special seven-man grand jury called during Danville's civil rights demonstrations of 1963, Martin issued a lone dissent against the indictments of

First State Bank, Directors, 1919. Marker Q-44. (Virginia Center For Digital History)

protesters. First State Bank posted bond for nearly 20 jailed demonstrators.

Q-100   HIGH STREET BAPTIST CHURCH

At 630 High Street. In 1865 emancipated African Americans withdrew from First Baptist Church, where they had worshiped from the balcony, and founded a congregation later known as High Street Baptist Church. Members erected their first sanctuary here in 1873. Fire destroyed that structure and its replacement, constructed in 1878. The present Romanesque Revival church was built in 1901. High Street Baptist served as a base for organizers of the local civil rights movement and hosted the Rev. Dr. Martin Luther King Jr. in 1963. Pastor Lendell W. Chase was president of the Danville Christian Progressive Association, which coordinated nonviolent protests against segregation and discrimination.

Q-7-d   HOLBROOK-ROSS HISTORIC DISTRICT

At the intersection of Holbrook and Ross Streets. The Holbrook-Ross Historic District, named for two major streets, is significant as the first neighborhood in Danville for African American professionals. Lawyers, ministers, dentists and physicians, as well as, business owners, insurance agents, postal clerks, and skilled craftsmen, made it their home in the late 19th century. It grew rapidly during the 1880s following the construction of the Danville School, the city's public school for blacks. By the turn of the 20th century, Holbrook Street had become Danville's foremost black residential address. The district is listed on the National Register of Historic Places and the Virginia Landmarks Register.

Q-5-c LOYAL BAPTIST CHURCH

On Loyal Street between Lynn and Court Streets.   The Loyal Street Baptist Church congregation, which was organized between 1865 and 1866 on Old Hospital-Dance Hill by former slaves, built its church here in 1870. Worship continued at this site until 1924 when the congregation moved to Holbrook Street. The name was then changed to Loyal Baptist Church.

Q-5-c PETERS PARK

On Foster Street between Betts and Branch Streets.   James Peters Sr. (ca. 1883-1970) opened Peters Park, also called the Almagro Baseball Stadium, at this site in 1948. The park was home to the Danville All-Stars, an African American baseball team that Peters sponsored. The stadium was state of the art when it opened, being one of the first in the country to boast lights to permit nighttime usage. Peters Park became an important part of the African American community, hosting Sunday afternoon baseball games as well as community events. In 1952 the park closed because of the racial integration of baseball and the ability to watch the sport on television.

Q-5-j WENDELL O. SCOTT SR. (1921–1990)

On Wendell Scott Drive between Arnett Boulevard and Locust Lane.   On 1 Dec. 1963 in Jacksonville, Florida, Wendell O. Scott Sr. became the first African American to win a NASCAR Grand National race. He lived here in the house he built after his return from World War II. Persevering over prejudice and discrimination, Scott broke racial barriers in the sport of NASCAR, with a 13-year career that included 20 top five and 147 top ten finishes. He retired in 1973 after an injury suffered during a race in Talladega, Alabama. The International Motorsports Hall of Fame, among 13 halls of fame, has inducted him as a member.

CITY OF EMPORIA

UM-48 JOHN DAY

On N. Main Street at the intersection with Valley Street.   John Day, a free African American cabinetmaker and brother of Thomas Day, cabinetmaker and builder, was born in Hicksford (present-day Emporia) on 18 Feb. 1797. Licensed in 1821 as a Baptist minister, he sailed in December 1830 to Liberia, where in 1853 he became pastor of Providence Church in Monrovia, the capital. In 1854 he established Day's Hope High School. He was a delegate to Liberia's constitutional convention, a signer of its constitution and its Declaration of Independence in 1847, and the second chief justice of its supreme court. Day died in Monrovia on 15 Feb. 1859.

FRANKLIN COUNTY

KP-14   BOOKER T. WASHINGTON
BIRTHPLACE

*On Booker T. Washington Highway (Rte.
122) approximately 600 feet north of
entrance to Booker T. Washington National
Monument.*   Booker T. Washington was
born a slave on the nearby Burroughs
plantation on April 5, 1856. He was graduated from Hampton Institute in 1875
where he became an instructor. Because
of his achievements as an educator, he
was selected to establish a normal school
for blacks in Alabama which later became
the Tuskegee Institute. Recognized as an
orator and author of *Up From Slavery*, he
exerted great influence both in the Republican party and as a humanitarian for
the benefit of his fellow blacks. He died
November 14, 1915.

HALIFAX COUNTY

U-53   HENRIETTA LACKS   (1920–1951)

*James D. Hagood Highway (Rte. 360)
approximately 100 feet west of Guill Town
Road (Rte. 720).*   Born in Roanoke on 1
Aug. 1920, Henrietta Pleasant lived here
with relatives after her mother's 1924
death. She married David Lacks in 1941
and, like many other African Americans,
moved to Baltimore, MD for wartime
employment. She died of cervical cancer
on 4 Oct. 1951. Cell tissue was removed
without permission (as usual then) for
medical research. Her cells multiplied
and survived at an extraordinarily high
rate, and are renowned worldwide as
the "HeLa line," the "gold standard" of
cell lines. Jonas Salk developed his polio
vaccine with them. Henrietta Lacks,
who in death saved countless lives, is
buried nearby.

LUNENBURG COUNTY

SN-70   LUNENBURG HIGH SCHOOL

*On K-V Road (Rte. 40) approximately 500
feet east of School Road.*   African American
patrons, lacking facilities for secondary education, established Lunenburg
Training School here about 1920. The
school benefited from the support of the
Jeanes Fund, which sponsored African
American supervisors of education in rural
southern communities. In 1924-25, the
Julius Rosenwald Fund contributed $900
for a larger school building. Rosenwald's
program, which helped build schools for
African Americans across the South, later
donated $400 for a shop. The county con-
structed a brick building here in 1949, and
the school was renamed Lunenburg High
School in 1951. When county schools were
desegregated in 1969, the building became
Lunenburg Junior High School.

SN-40   NATHANIEL LEE HAWTHORNE
(1923–1975)

*In Victoria on Mecklenburg Avenue at inter-
section with W. 10th Street.*   Nathaniel Lee
Hawthorne, civil rights leader, campaigned
for racial and social justice for the people
of Southside Virginia. A native of Lunenburg County and a World War II veteran,
he conducted his work despite death
threats and other attempts at intimidation.
Operating from the "Freedom House" in
Victoria, Hawthorne chaired the Lunenburg branch of the NAACP from 1965 to
1974 and was a coordinator of the Virginia
Students' Civil Rights Committee. He led
efforts to desegregate schools, register
voters, gain equal access to restaurants
and stores, and secure African American
representation in local government. In
1965 he organized a voting rights march
that passed along this route.

CITY OF LYNCHBURG

Q-6-30   AMELIA PERRY PRIDE'S DORCHESTER HOME

On Pierce Street between 13th and 14th Streets.   Near this spot stood a small frame house known as Dorchester Home or Old Folks Home for impoverished former slave women. Established in 1897 by Hampton Institute graduate and Lynchburg public school principal Amelia Perry Pride (1857-1932), it provided shelter, fuel, clothing, and food for its residents until their deaths. Following Hampton Institute's principle of uplifting her race through self-help, Pride was a passionate advocate of African American and Virginia Indian education. In Lynchburg, she provided scholarships for many young women seeking higher education and established sewing and cooking schools for women and men entering vocational fields.

Q-6-28   C. W. SEAY   (CA. 1900–1982)

On Pierce Street between 13th and 14th Streets.   Clarence William "Dick" Seay, who lived here, was principal of Dunbar High School, Lynchburg's secondary school for African Americans. A pioneer in the struggle for equal opportunities for blacks, for 30 years Seay shaped Dunbar High School into a school of academic excellence, holding that a "successful school and its community are inseparable." He later became the first high school principal elected to the presidency of the Association of Colleges and Secondary Schools. After his retirement in 1968, Seay taught at Lynchburg College and served two terms as Lynchburg's first black city council member since the 1880s and the first black vice mayor.

Q-6-29   CAMP DAVIS

On Pierce Street between 12th and 13th Streets.   Camp Davis, a Civil War mustering ground for Confederate troops from Virginia under the command of Col. Jubal A. Early, once occupied this area. At least 130 Southern soldiers died at the camp's own Pratt Hospital and were buried in Lynchburg's Old City Cemetery. The neighborhood's historically African American identity took shape during Reconstruction, when Camp Davis became an important refuge for freed slaves. Before being annexed by the city in 1870, it was the site of Federal military headquarters, the Freedmen's Bureau's Camp Davis School, headed by Jacob Eschbach Yoder, and a black Methodist Episcopal church.

Q-6-23   CHAUNCEY E. SPENCER, SR.

On Pierce Street between 13th and 14th Streets.   Chauncey E. Spencer, Sr., aviation pioneer and Civil Rights activist was born in Lynchburg on 5 Nov. 1906, the son of poet Anne Spencer. He moved to Chicago and by 1934 began pursuing his pilot's license. As a charter member of the National Airmen's Association of America, he and Dale L. White in 1939 made an aeronautical tour from Chicago to Washington, D.C., to lobby for the inclusion of African Americans in the Army Air Corps. This included meeting Senator Harry S Truman. Spencer also worked for the U.S. Air Force and was a public servant in Michigan and California. He lived here from 1977 until his death on 21 Aug. 2002.

Q-18   COURT STREET BAPTIST CHURCH

At 517 Court Street.   The congregation was organized in 1843, when Lynchburg's African American Baptists were separated from First Baptist Church. The new African Baptist Church of Lynchburg met in a converted theater. It was demolished in 1879, after the deaths of eight people

Chauncy E. Spencer (left), his mother Anne Spencer, and Dale L. White standing next to the bi-plane flown cross country, at Preston Glenn Airport, Lynchburg, 1939. Markers Q-6-23 and Q-6-20. (University of Michigan Library Digital Collections. Bentley Image Bank)

during a panic caused by fear of structural collapse. Church members provided all the money to buy land at Sixth and Court Street for a new building. Local architect Robert C. Burkholder designed the church, combining the Romanesque Revival and Second Empire styles. It was the largest church building with the tallest spire in the city in 1880.

Q-7   DIAMOND HILL BAPTIST CHURCH

At 1415 E. Grace Street.   Diamond Hill Baptist Church was established in 1872, seven years after slavery was abolished. The current church, a Gothic Revival–style building, was completed in 1886. Under the pastorate and leadership of the Rev. Dr. Virgil A. Wood from 1958 to 1963, the church became central to the Civil Rights movement in the Lynchburg area as the base of operations for demonstrations, sit-ins, and rallies seeking to end segregation. The church also hosted speeches by notable figures in the national Civil Rights movement. Efforts to achieve racial equality continued under the 1964–2000 pastorate of the Rev. Dr. Haywood Robinson Jr.

Q-6-27   DR. ROBERT WALTER JOHNSON (1899–1971)

On Pierce Street, between 14th and 15th Streets.   The desegregation of tennis was due in large part to the efforts of Dr. Robert W. "Whirlwind" Johnson. The first African American to earn staff privileges at Lynchburg General Hospital, he also worked to overcome barriers keeping young African Americans out of tennis. As founder of the Junior Development Program of the American Tennis Association, Johnson sponsored African-American players from across the country in tournaments, and coached and mentored them on backyard courts here at his home. Among those he trained were Wimbledon Champions Althea Gibson and Arthur Ashe. Johnson was posthumously inducted into the International Tennis Hall of Fame in 2009.

Q-13   JACOB E. YODER

At intersection of Jackson and 2nd Streets. Jacob Eschbach Yoder (22 Feb. 1838–15 Apr. 1905), reared a Mennonite in Pennsylvania, came to Lynchburg after the Civil War to teach former slaves in the Freedmen's Bureau's Camp Davis School. Following Reconstruction, Yoder served as supervising principal of Lynchburg's

African American schools for more than 25 years and helped start the College Hill Baptist Church Sunday school. When he died, black teachers declared that "he had devoted his life unselfishly, and unstintingly to our race, and wore himself out in service to us." In 1911, the Lynchburg School Board named the new Yoder School for blacks, which stood here, after this public school pioneer.

Q-6-21 LUKE JORDAN, BLUES PIONEER

On Jefferson Street at intersection with Horseford Road. Singer-guitarist Luke Jordan (1892–1952) was a familiar presence on the streets of Lynchburg from the 1920s until World War II. Jordan and other African American musicians in the Southeast merged blues with an existing repertoire of ballads, ragtime, and tent-show songs, creating a syncopated and upbeat style now called Piedmont or East Coast Blues. The Victor Record Company, seeking blues artists to satisfy popular demand, recorded Jordan in 1927 and 1929, issuing classics such as "Church Bell Blues" and "Pick Poor Robin Clean." The Great Depression hurt sales and ended Jordan's career, but he remained an important and widely imitated Virginia blues musician.

Q-6-46 MEGGINSON ROSENWALD SCHOOL

At 136 Spinoza Circle. The Megginson School was built here ca. 1923 for African American students in the Pleasant Valley community, then part of Campbell County. Albert Megginson (1831-1923), formerly enslaved, purchased land in this area after the Civil War and later donated two acres for the school. The two-classroom building was constructed with financial support from local African Americans, the county, and the Julius Rosenwald Fund, which helped build more than 5,000 schools and supporting structures for black students in the rural South between 1917 and 1932. African American resident Wiley Gaines purchased school buses that transported students to this and other local segregated schools.

Q-6-25 OLD CITY CEMETERY

On Taylor Street at intersection with 4th Street. Old City Cemetery, also known as the Methodist Cemetery, was established as a public burial ground in 1806 on land donated by John Lynch, founder of Lynchburg. Mayors and other prominent civic leaders, along with the city's indigent and "strangers," are among the estimated 20,000 people buried here. Three quarters of those interred here are of African descent, both enslaved and free. The cemetery's Confederate section contains the graves of more than 2,200 soldiers from 14 states. Museums on the property interpret the diverse history of this rehabilitated graveyard and its inhabitants. The cemetery was listed on the National Register of Historic Places in 1973.

Q-6-39 OTA BENGA (CA. 1885–1916)

On Dewitt Street at intersection with Garfield Avenue. Mbye Otabenga, later known as Ota Benga, was born in what is now the Democratic Republic of the Congo. In 1904 the Rev. Samuel P. Verner, adventurer and former Presbyterian missionary, brought Benga and eight other Congolese purported to be "Pygmies" to be displayed at the St. Louis World's Fair. Two years later the Bronx Zoo in New York exhibited Benga in its "Monkey House" alongside an orangutan. Outraged African American ministers secured his release from the zoo and placed him in an orphanage in Brooklyn. In 1910 Benga was brought to Lynchburg to attend the Virginia Theological Seminary and College. Despondent over his inability to return to Africa, he committed suicide in 1916.

Q-6-35 PAUL LAURENCE DUNBAR HIGH
SCHOOL

At 1200 Polk Street. African American
community leaders petitioned Lynchburg's school board for a new high school
to serve black students early in the
1920s. Named for poet Paul Laurence
Dunbar, the school opened here in 1923.
Shop, home economics, and administration buildings were later constructed.
Clarence W. Seay, principal from 1938 to
1968, recruited a dedicated faculty and
expanded the curriculum. Counselor
Pauline Weeden Maloney guided many
graduates to major universities. The
school's cultural, literary, and athletic
programs made it a focal point for the
African American community. Dunbar
became a junior high school in 1970-71,
and the original building was demolished in 1979.

Q-6-31 PAULINE WEEDEN MALONEY
(1904–1987)

*On Buchanan Street between 13th and 14th
Streets.* Here lived Pauline Maloney,
known as Lynchburg's "first lady of education." A graduate of Howard University,
she worked in Lynchburg public schools
from 1937 to 1970, most notably as a
guidance counselor and administrator at
the all-black Dunbar High School. During
the 1970s she was elected the first black
president of both the Virginia School
Boards Association and the National
School Boards Association Southern
Region. In 1977 Maloney became the first
woman rector of Norfolk State University.
She served as national president of The
Links, Inc., a civic organization of African
American women, and she founded the
Lynchburg chapter in 1950.

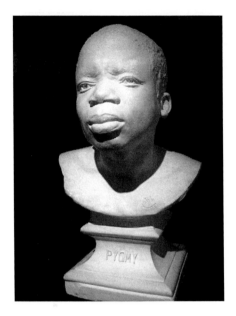

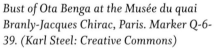

*Bust of Ota Benga at the Musée du quai
Branly-Jacques Chirac, Paris. Marker Q-6-
39. (Karl Steel: Creative Commons)*

Q-6-26 PROFESSOR FRANK TRIGG
(1850–1933)

*On Pierce Street between 13th and 14th
Streets.* Frank Trigg was a leading black
educator in Virginia. He was born into
slavery in Richmond while his parents
were personal servants of Virginia Governor John B. Floyd. After the Civil War he
attended Hampton Institute, and began
teaching in Abingdon before moving to
Lynchburg in 1880. He was a teacher and
principal here for 22 years and became
the first black supervisor of Lynchburg's
black public schools. He was co-founder
of the Virginia Teachers' Association, and
later was president of colleges in Virginia,
Maryland and North Carolina. In 1926 he
retired to Lynchburg and resided here. He
is buried in Old City Cemetery.

Q-6-20   THE ANNE SPENCER HOUSE—1313 PIERCE STREET

At 1313 Pierce Street.   This was the home of Edward Alexander and Anne Bannister Spencer from 1903 until her death on July 25, 1975. Born on February 6, 1882, in Henry County, Va. Anne Spencer was to receive national and international recognition as a poet. Published extensively between 1920 and 1935, she belonged to the Harlem Renaissance school of writers.

Q-6-38   VIRGINIA COLLEGIATE AND INDUSTRIAL INSTITUTE

On Seabury Avenue in front of Bass Elementary School.   The Virginia Collegiate and Industrial Institute opened here in 1893 as a branch of Morgan College in Baltimore, Maryland. The school offered college preparation, industrial education, and teacher training to African American students. Jackson Street Methodist Episcopal Church in Lynchburg purchased land for the campus and provided additional financial support. The Freedmen's Aid Society of the Methodist Episcopal Church contributed funds for operating expenses. African American educator Frank Trigg was the institute's first principal. After a fire destroyed the main building in Dec. 1917, the school closed and its students were transferred to Morgan College in Baltimore.

Q-6-41   VIRGINIA TEACHERS ASSOCIATION

At 901 Jackson Street.   African American educators organized the Virginia Teachers' Reading Circle here at the Jackson Street Methodist Episcopal Church on 13 Aug. 1887. Established during a session of the Peabody Normal Institute, a summer course for teachers from across the state, the Reading Circle provided professional development for teachers of black students in Virginia's public schools. James Hugo Johnston, second president of what is now Virginia State University, was elected to lead the organization. Later known as the Virginia Teachers Association, the group served black educators until it merged with the Virginia Education Association on 1 Jan. 1967.

Q-6-15   VIRGINIA UNIVERSITY OF LYNCHBURG

On Dewitt Street at intersection with Garfield Avenue.   In 1886 the Virginia Baptist State Convention founded the Lynchburg Baptist Seminary as an institution of "self-reliance," "racial pride," and "faith". It first offered classes in 1890 as the renamed Virginia Seminary. Under the direction of Gregory Willis Hayes, the second president of the college who served from 1891 to 1906, the school became a pioneer in the field of African American education. In 1900 the school was reincorporated as the Virginia Theological Seminary and College and in 1962 became the Virginia Seminary and College. The college was renamed and incorporated as Virginia University of Lynchburg in 1996. Among its graduates was the poet Anne Spencer.

CITY OF MARTINSVILLE

A-107   FAYETTE STREET

On Fayette Street at intersection with Market Street.   Since the late 19th century, Fayette Street has been a gateway to the business, social, and cultural life of African Americans here. Institutions such as Mt. Zion A.M.E. Church (founded in 1870), St. Mary's Hospital (1926–1952), Piedmont Christian Institute (1900–1934), and Imperial Savings and Loan (founded in 1929) were pillars of this community. A part of the street known as Baldwin's Block

(1920s–1960s) represented the entrepreneurial spirit of the people. Dr. Dana O. Baldwin and his brothers founded the June German Ball, which was held at a number of venues here. This annual musical and dance festival hosted world-renowned African American musicians that played to regional audiences.

MECKLENBURG COUNTY

UL-8   James Solomon Russell (1857–1935)

On Rte. 1 approximately 200 feet north of Paschall Road (Rte. 712).   James Solomon Russell was born enslaved on 20 Dec. 1857 on the nearby Hendrick Plantation. After emancipation, he attended Hampton Institute and St. Stephen's Normal and Theological School and was ordained in 1882. As a religious missionary, Russell established nearly 30 churches. He also founded the St. Paul Normal and Industrial Institute (Saint Paul's College) in Lawrenceville in 1882 and was its principal until 1929. In 1892, Russell became Archdeacon for Colored Work in the Diocese of Southern Virginia. Inspired by Booker T. Washington, he started an annual farmers' conference in 1904. Russell urged African Americans to stay out of debt, vote, and become land owners.

Z-159   Mecklenburg County Training School

In South Hill at Meadow Street 200 feet east of Brook Avenue.   In 1915, four influential African American residents of South Hill—the Rev. J. H. Simmons, Mary E. Simmons, Robert Walker, and James E. Skipwith—established the Mecklenburg County Training School for black students. The school operated in the True Reformer Lodge Hall for three terms before a two-room frame building

was constructed in 1918. Matilda M. Booker, Jeanes supervisor of black teachers in 1920, secured $1,500 from the Rosenwald Fund and encouraged parents to raise another $3,000 for a new school building. With the county's aid, the 500-student school was completed near here in 1925. It burned in 1942.

U-95   Patrick Robert "Parker" Sydnor   (1854–1950)

On Rte. 49 between Rte. 15 and Wilbourne Road (Rte. 701).   Born enslaved on one of William Sydnor's plantations in Halifax County, Patrick Robert "Parker" Sydnor became literate at a freedmen's school after the Civil War. A preacher and farmer in his youth, he began crafting grave markers in the 1890s and remained active until the 1940s. Sydnor won renown as a skilled stonecutter and engraver who made his work widely accessible. His designs and inscriptions memorialized the lives of African Americans across Southside Virginia. His home, the nearby Patrick Robert "Parker" Sydnor log cabin, is listed on the Virginia Landmarks Register and the National Register of Historic Places.

U-81   Thyne Institute

At 5450 Highway Forty Seven.   In 1876 the United Presbyterian Church and the Rev. J. J. Ashenhurst, first principal, formed Thyne Institute, the only facility in Mecklenburg County offering courses for blacks until 1923. Two years after opening in a small building that had been used for curing tobacco, the school moved to a new building that John Thyne, for whom the school was named, had erected on five acres of land. The Institute grew in time into a boarding school and later into a four-year high school. Purchased by the Mecklenburg County School Board in 1946, the site presently serves as Chase City Elementary School.

Oliver White Hill, Sr. Markers M-36, SA-8, and K-91. (The Oliver White Hill Foundation)

U-94   WEST END HIGH SCHOOL

On Rte. 49 approximately 200 feet south of intersection with Middle School Road. Just to the east is the former West End High School, which served African Americans during the segregation era. With the help of Matilda M. Booker, Mecklenburg County's Jeanes Fund supervisor of education for blacks, local parents first established the school in Clarksville in 1935. In 1951, the U.S. government purchased the West End property for the development of Buggs Island Lake. Using state funds set aside for a major school-construction initiative under Gov. John S. Battle, the county built a new West End High School, which opened here in 1953. The last class graduated in 1969, when the building became a junior high school.

MONTGOMERY COUNTY

K-68   CHRISTIANSBURG INDUSTRIAL INSTITUTE

In Christiansburg on N. Franklin Street (Rte. 460 Bus.) between Scattergood Drive NE and Church Street NE. In 1866, Captain Charles S. Schaeffer, a Freedmen's Bureau agent, organized a school for blacks on the hill just to the southeast. Charles L. Marshall of Tuskegee Institute became principal of the school in 1896. Under his guidance and with support from Philadelphia Quakers, a library, dormitories, classrooms, shops, and barns were constructed. Both academic and industrial classes were offered at the institute until 1947 when it became a public high school. In 1966, the institute graduated its last class, and its property was sold at public auction.

NOTTOWAY COUNTY

K-315   NOTTOWAY TRAINING SCHOOL

In Blackstone on Rocky Bump Road (Rte. 668) at intersection with Epes Street. On this site stood the Nottoway Training School, the first public school to provide secondary education for African Americans in Nottoway County. In 1909, public appeals to raise funds led to the establishment of the school by 1913, making it one of the first training schools for African Americans opened in the Commonwealth. The John F. Slater Fund helped finance teachers' salaries. County training schools were built to provide rural students vocational and agricultural education, as well as to prepare them for teaching careers or college. Nottoway Training School became an accredited high school in 1931. It closed in 1950 when the Luther H. Foster High School opened.

PRINCE EDWARD COUNTY

M-35 BLANCHE KELSO BRUCE

On Patrick Henry Highway (Rte. 360) at intersection with Tower Road (Rte. 623). Blanche Kelso Bruce, African American political leader, was born into slavery south of here on 1 Mar. 1841. He grew up in Virginia, Mississippi, and Missouri before escaping slavery during the Civil War. In 1869 Bruce moved back to Mississippi and became active in local and state politics. In Feb. 1874, the Mississippi legislature elected him to the U.S. Senate. Bruce was the first black to serve a full term in the Senate (1875-1881). After completing his term in office, he held several political positions in Washington, D.C. He died on 17 Mar. 1898 in Washington, D.C., and was interred there in Woodlawn Cemetery.

M-29 CCC COMPANY 1390 CAMP GALLION

On Patrick Henry Highway (Rte. 360) at intersection with Tower Road (Rte. 623). A short distance west is the site of Camp Gallion, home from 1933 to 1941 of Civilian Conservation Corps Company 1390. This all-African American company performed extensive work in the present-day Prince Edward–Gallion State Forest. Company 1390 built five forest-fire lookout towers, 94 miles of forest-fire lanes, 62 miles of truck trails, 33 bridges, and both Goodwin and Prince Edward Lakes, now the centerpieces of Twin Lakes State Park. The men also thinned 500 acres of forest, planted 4,500 trees, and performed 3,142 hours of fire-fighting duty. In addition, the company conducted an education program to reduce illiteracy among its members.

I-14-A FREE BLACKS OF ISRAEL HILL

In Farmville on Layne Street at intersection with W. 3rd Street (Rte. 15/460 Bus.). To the west lies Israel Hill, settled in 1810–1811 by approximately ninety formerly enslaved persons who received freedom and 350 acres from Judith Randolph under the will of her husband, Richard Randolph, cousin of Thomas Jefferson. These "Israelites" and other free African Americans worked as farmers, craftspeople, and Appomattox River boatmen; some labored alongside whites for equal wages and defended their rights in court. The family of early settler Hercules White bought and sold real estate in Farmville and joined with white citizens to found the town's first Baptist church in 1836. Israel Hill remained a vigorous black community into the twentieth century.

I-26 MARTHA E. FORRESTER (1863–1951)

In Farmville at 501 Race Street. Martha E. Forrester lived in this house. In 1920 she helped establish the Council of Colored Women to foster community uplift. As the organization's president for 31 years, she led its campaigns to improve educational opportunities for African American students in Prince Edward County, securing a longer school term and higher-level courses. She was instrumental in convincing the county to build its first high school for African Americans, which opened in 1939 and was named for educator Robert Russa Moton. The Martha E. Forrester Council of Women, renamed in her honor, later played a central role in establishing the Moton Museum to interpret the history of civil rights in education.

M-36 OLIVER WHITE HILL SR. (1907–2007)

In Farmville at S. Main Street (Rte. 15 Bus.) and Griffin Boulevard. On behalf of local plaintiffs, civil rights attorney

Oliver White Hill Sr. and law partners Martin A. Martin and Spottswood Robinson III filed *Davis v. Prince Edward* in 1951 to challenge racial segregation in public schools. This case, along with several others consolidated into *Brown v. Board*, led to the U.S. Supreme Court's 1954 decision declaring public school segregation unconstitutional. Defying a desegregation order in 1959, Prince Edward County closed its public schools. Hill and NAACP leaders Roy Wilkins and L. Francis Griffin led a rally at the county courthouse in 1961 denouncing the closings. Schools reopened in 1964 as ordered by the Supreme Court in *Griffin v. Prince Edward*.

M-23 PRINCE EDWARD STATE PARK FOR NEGROES

On Patrick Henry Highway (Rte. 360) approximately 500 feet east of Twin Lakes Road (Rte. 621). Prince Edward State Park for Negroes was established in 1950 one mile west on the site of the former Prince Edward Lake Recreation Area for Negroes. Maceo C. Martin, an African American from Danville, sued the state when he was denied access to Staunton River State Park. Governor William M. Tuck funded the new park to provide "similar and equal" facilities in lieu of access. The park, with a black superintendent, was operated separately from neighboring Goodwin Lake Recreation Area until the passage of the Civil Rights Act of 1964. The two parks merged in 1986 to form Twin Lakes State Park.

M-1   ROBERT RUSSA MOTON HIGH SCHOOL

In Farmville at S. Main Street (Rte. 15 Bus.) and Griffin Boulevard.   On this site 4-23-51, the students staged a strike protesting inadequate school facilities. Led by Rev. L. Francis Griffin, these

students' actions became a part of the 1954 U.S. Supreme Court's *Brown v. Board of Education* decision, which ruled racial segregation in public schools unconstitutional. To avoid desegregation, the Prince Edward County public schools were closed until 9-2-64.

M-30   SULPHUR SPRING BAPTIST CHURCH

On Sulphur Spring Road (Rte. 657) at intersection with Rte. 615. According to local tradition, the Sulphur Spring Baptist Church was founded in 1867, when services were held in a brush arbor. During the Reconstruction period, formerly enslaved African Americans formed congregations throughout the South similar to this church. By 1876 a log structure had been built and in that year the congregation purchased the one-acre tract of land on which it stood. The founding members of the church included Phillip Harris, William Wright, Alex Scott, William Green, and Daniel Carter. The first frame structure was built in 1900 and used until 1914 when the original part of the current church was constructed.

M-27   VERNON JOHNS

On Darlington Heights Road (Rte. 665) at intersection with Douglas Church Road (Rte. 666). Rev. Dr. Vernon Johns was born here in Darlington Heights on 22 April 1892. A graduate of Oberlin College, Johns was an orator of great renown and the first African-American minister included in Best Sermons of the Year (1926), an international publication. He was pastor of Court Street Baptist Church (1920-1926; 1941-1943) and president of Virginia Theological Seminary and College (1929-1934), both in Lynchburg. Later he was pastor of Dexter Avenue Baptist Church in Montgomery, Alabama (1948-1952). A blunt-spoken opponent of racial segregation and a champion of civil rights, Johns exhorted his congregations to resist the laws that constricted their lives. He died in Washington, D.C., on 10 June 1965, and is buried just north of here.

CITY OF RADFORD

K-330 LOVELY MOUNT BAPTIST CHURCH

On the campus of Radford University on Fairfax Street between Peters Hall and Adams Street.   On 13 Nov. 1869, the Rev. Capt. Charles S. Schaeffer of the Bureau of Refugees, Freedmen, and Abandoned Lands met with the people of Lovely Mount (later Radford) and organized the Lovely Mount Baptist Church. In 1898, the congregation purchased the Lutheran church that stood at this location on Fairfax Street, and changed its name to the First Baptist Church. The first church of the Baptist denomination in Radford, Lovely Mount/First Baptist Church served the African American community for more than 60 years until Radford College purchased it in 1961 and demolished it to expand Peters Hall.

CITY OF ROANOKE

K-99 MOUNT MORIAH BAPTIST CHURCH

*At 3521 E. Orange Avenue NE (Rte. 460/221).*The members of Mount Moriah Baptist Church belong to one of the region's earliest African American congregations, originating in a Sunday school for slaves established in the mid-1800s by Dr. Charles L. Cocke, founder of Hollins College. The group gained permission in 1858 to build its first church. The present church, the congregation's third, was built about 1908. It was added to the National Register of Historic Places and the Virginia Landmarks Register in 1994. The nearby cemetery was expanded from a former slave burial ground.

K-91 OLIVER WHITE HILL SR. (1909–2007)

On Gilmer Avenue NW at intersection with 4th Street NW.   Oliver White Hill Sr., Presidential Medal of Freedom honoree, worked to dismantle Jim Crow laws in the United States. Over his nearly seven-decade career as a civil rights attorney, Hill challenged inequities in education, employment, and public facilities. With law partner Spottswood W. Robinson III, Hill argued *Davis v. Prince Edward County*, one of four cases consolidated into the 1954 U.S. Supreme Court decision *Brown v. Board*. Hill lived here at 401 Gilmer Avenue NW with Lelia and Bradford Pentecost from 1913-1923. After completing high school, college, and law school in Washington, DC, he returned to Roanoke's Gainsboro community in 1934 to practice law. Hill settled in Richmond in 1939.

K-90 OSCAR MICHEAUX   (1884–1951)

On Henry Street NW at intersection with Loudon Avenue NW. Oscar Micheaux, renowned leading creator of African American "race films" between 1919 and 1948, produced up to six full-length films in Roanoke between 1922 and 1925. The Strand Theatre housed the Micheaux Film Corporation from 1923 to 1925, while Micheaux lodged across the street at the Hampton Hotel, now the Dumas. Many of Roanoke's black professionals bought stock in Micheaux's corporation and five served on its board of directors including Alfred F. Brooks, who built the Strand. Famous civil rights attorney Oliver W. Hill, Sr., then a student boarding in Roanoke, had a walk-on part in one film.

Lobby card for Oscar Micheaux's production of "The Notorius Elinor Lee". Marker K-90. (New York Public Library Digital Collections)

WISE COUNTY

KA-17 Carl Martin—Early Musical Pioneer

In Big Stone Gap at the Harry W. Meador Jr. Coal Museum on E. 3rd Street N at the intersection with Shawnee Avenue E. Carl Martin was born in Big Stone Gap in April 1906. He grew up in Southwest Virginia and moved to Knoxville, Tenn., in 1918. He performed regionally on the guitar, mandolin, bass, and violin at coal camps, dances, and in traveling shows. In 1930, Martin's string band recorded two instrumentals for Vocalion, released under the band name "Tennessee Chocolate Drops" for a black audience and the "Tennessee Trio" in the white old-time music series. Martin moved to Chicago in the 1930s, recording blues and performing with such artists as Big Bill Broonzy and Tampa Red until serving in World War II. The 1960s folk revival brought Martin before new audiences. He died in Detroit on 10 May 1979.

WYTHE COUNTY

K-325 Wytheville Training School

In Wytheville at the African American Heritage Museum, 410 E. Franklin Street. By 1867, the Freedmen's Bureau began educating African Americans recently freed from enslavement in Wytheville and soon a building was constructed for the students. In 1882, the Evansham School District and the Franklin Street Methodist Episcopal Church purchased the Freedmen's School and erected a larger school here that became known as the Wytheville Training School. By the late 1940s the school provided secondary school education to African American students from Wythe, Bland, Carroll, and Grayson Counties, as well. The school closed in 1951. The following year a new building opened—Scott Memorial High School—in memory of Richard Henry Scott, an early black educator in the region.

Acknowledgments

Virginia's historical marker program has been the work of scholars, editorial committees, program managers, sponsors, board members, and government administrators for ninety-one years. As the program enters its tenth decade, the journey undertaken to tell the full story of our commonwealth is still unfinished. Much remains to be said about the people, places, and events significant in Virginia's past, and DHR is fully mindful that the story will continue to unfold as each new generation ventures forth.

This project would not have happened without the contributions made by the many individuals and organizations that have proposed and funded the creation of new markers. DHR is grateful for their invaluable financial support, and especially for their patience as the wheel that turns proposed topics into concise and academically accurate texts slowly revolves. Not every topic proposed meets the criteria of statewide significance, and it is always difficult to explain why that is to people who are justifiably proud of the history they wish to document via the marker program. Fortunately, there are many localities in Virgina that maintain local historical marker programs specifically for this purpose, and DHR hopes that they and the state's program will continue to flourish.

The Virginia Department of Transportation (VDOT) is an essential partner in the program. Without the expertise of its staff it would be impossible to safely locate, erect, and maintain the thousands of markers in the inventory. We are also grateful for the local public works departments that perform these functions in jurisdictions outside VDOT authority. Acknowledgment must be made to the many historians who have volunteered to serve on the editorial committee that works with the program's manager to prepare texts for presentation to the Virginia Board of Historic Resources (BHR). The Board's encouragement and support for the program, and ultimately its review and approval of newly proposed markers, is greatly appreciated. So, too, is the support of DHR's director, Julie V. Langan, who is equally dedicated to the program's important mission, and fully grasps its meaning to both Virginians and the thousands of visitors who come to experience one of the commonwealth's most valuable assets—its hundreds of years of history. Dr. Colita Nichols Fairfax, the vice-chair of the BHR, contributed the foreword for this publication, and my colleagues and I greatly appreciate the generous donation of her time. DHR's public affairs officer, Randy Jones, is also to be credited for shepherding this work through the production process, as well as for diligently promoting the program through a constant flow of informative press releases.

Personally I would like to give special thanks to the staff of the Division of Survey and Register at DHR. It is only through their skill and dedication that extra time can be found to add special projects such as this book to the daily responsibilities of the Division. Ultimately, however, it is program manager Jennifer Loux and researcher Matt Gottlieb who are to be acknowledged for making this project possible. Theirs is a daunting remit, the challenges of which they never fail to meet—thank you.

JAMES K. HARE
Director, Division of Survey and Register
Virginia Department of Historic Resources

Index